ACADEMIC
ENCOUNTERS

CONTENT
FOCUS
Human Behavior

ACADEMIC ENCOUNTERS

Reading, Study Skills, and Writing

Teacher's Manual

CONTENT
FOCUS
Human Behavior

BERNARD SEAL

CAMBRIDGE
UNIVERSITY PRESS

PUBLISHED BY THE PRESS SYNDICATE OF THE UNIVERSITY OF CAMBRIDGE
The Pitt Building, Trumpington Street, Cambridge CB2 1RP, United Kingdom

CAMBRIDGE UNIVERSITY PRESS
The Edinburgh Building, Cambridge CB2 2RU, United Kingdom
40 West 20th Street, New York, NY 10011–4211, USA
10 Stamford Road, Oakleigh, Melbourne 3166, Australia

© Cambridge University Press 1997

First published 1997

Printed in the United States of America

Typeset in New Aster

ISBN 0 521 47660 7 Teacher's Manual
ISBN 0 521 47658 5 Student's Book

Book design and text composition by Jill Little, *Mediamark*

Copyright

Contents

Introduction

ANSWERS TO QUESTIONS COMMONLY ASKED ABOUT *ACADEMIC ENCOUNTERS*

Who is the book aimed at?

Academic Encounters: Reading, Study Skills, and Writing is written for the student who has either just started or is about to start attending a community college or university in an English-speaking environment. Ideally, this student should be entering an undergraduate program, although a graduate student who has never been exposed to academic English will also benefit from using this book. The student's English language proficiency can range from high intermediate to low advanced. Even students who are native speakers (or who immigrated at an early age) can benefit from using this book, since it prepares students for the types of texts and tasks that they will encounter in the college environment.

What approach is adopted and why?

Academic Encounters adopts a content-based approach to the study of academic English. Students are presented with authentic samples of text taken from North American college textbooks. They read through the texts seemingly with the prime purpose of understanding the content. In fact, as students work through the book they are also learning reading and study skills, and test preparation strategies. Additionally, the texts are used for language study, so students become familiar with the vocabulary and structures used in academic discourse.

Each unit of *Academic Encounters* focuses on some aspect of human behavior. The fact that the book has a unified thematic content throughout has several advantages. First, it gives the students a realistic sense of studying a course at a university, in which each week's assignments are related to and build on each other. Second, as language and concepts recur, the students begin to feel that the readings are getting easier, which helps to build their confidence as readers of academic text. Finally, after studying the book, some students may feel that they have enough background in the subject matter to take a course in psychology or human communications to fulfill part of their general education requirements.

The individual topics in *Academic Encounters* were chosen for their appeal to students. It is important for students to be interested in what they are reading about and studying, and for them to be able to find personal connections to it. According to language acquisition theory, it can be argued that language development occurs more readily under such conditions. Similarly, it can be argued that the writing process is facilitated when students are well informed on a topic, have developed personal connections to it, and are engaged by it.

Are there many opportunities for student interaction?

Although *Academic Encounters* is a reading, study skills, and writing book, speaking activities abound. Students discuss the content of the texts before and after reading them; they often work collaboratively to solve task problems; they perform role-play activities; and they frequently compare answers in pairs or small groups.

How long does it take to teach Academic Encounters?

Academic Encounters contains five units of material. Each unit requires approximately 16–20 hours of instruction. *Academic Encounters* could thus be a suitable course for a 64- to 80-hour course (when a teacher selects four of the five units) or an 80- to 100-hour course (when all the units are used). The course, however, can be made shorter or longer. To shorten the course, you might choose not to do every task in the book and to assign some tasks and texts as homework, rather than as classwork. To lengthen the course, you might choose to supplement the book with some content-related materials from your own files and to spend more time developing students' writing skills.

Do the units have to be taught in order?

The units do not have to be taught in the order in which they appear in the book, although this order is recommended. To a certain extent, tasks do build upon each other so that, for example, a note-taking task later in the book may draw upon information that has been offered in an earlier unit. If you want to teach the units out of order, however, you may do so. You can use the task index at the back of the book to see what information has been presented in earlier units and build that information into your lesson. In terms of reading topics, also, the order of units is regarded as optimal, especially for students who have recently arrived in North America. Many of these students are under great stress and thus find the first unit particularly useful since it deals with how to manage stress and stay healthy. The final unit should only be covered when students feel comfortable with each other, since it deals with more intimate topics such as friendship and love.

What special design features does Academic Encounters have?

A great deal of attention has been paid to design features in *Academic Encounters*. There are two different types of pages: task pages and text pages. Tasks and texts never appear on the same page, and every new reading starts on a right-hand page faced by a left-hand page of prereading tasks. Task pages are clearly differentiated from text pages by a colored strip running along the outside edge.

One of the most important design features of the book is that the text pages have been formatted to look very much like pages in a college-level textbook. The two-thirds' width column of text found in many textbooks has been employed, and there are figures, diagrams, and tables spread throughout the texts.

Photographs or illustrations with captions appear on almost every text page. Key words are shown in boldface and specialized terms are given in italics. The words in boldface also appear in the margin with brief definitions.

What was the source material for the readings?

The five units of *Academic Encounters* are each based on material taken from either a psychology or human communications textbook that has been used in regular university or community college courses in North America. The textbook material has been abridged and occasionally re-organized, but on the sentence level little of the language has been changed.

GENERAL GUIDELINES FOR TEACHING THE DIFFERENT COMPONENTS OF *ACADEMIC ENCOUNTERS*

Each unit of *Academic Encounters: Reading, Study Skills, and Writing* contains these elements:

- Unit title page
- Previewing the Unit
- Two chapters, each containing four readings, each of which are divided into these sections:
    Preparing to Read
    Now Read
    After You Read
- Two chapter writing assignments (one at the end of each chapter)
- Unit content quiz (photocopiable pages found in the teacher's manual only)

The remainder of this section contains some general guidelines for teaching each element. See Units 1–5 in the body of this teacher's manual for more detailed information, and for specific ideas for teaching each text and task found in *Academic Encounters* (student's book).

Unit title page

Each unit starts with a unit title page that contains the title of the unit, a large illustration or photograph that is suggestive of the content of the unit, and a brief paragraph that summarizes the unit. This page is intended to look like a typical unit opening page in a university course book.

Naturally, this page is a good place to start the study of a new unit. You should look at the title of the unit with the students and make sure they understand what it means. Then look at the picture and have students describe it and attempt to relate it to the title.

One way to start each unit is to teach a lexical set that is relevant to the title and theme of the unit. For example, in starting Unit 2, Development Through Life, you could elicit and pre-teach the lexical set *baby, infant, boy, girl, teenager, adult,* and so on.

Finally, look briefly at the summary paragraph at the bottom of the page. Read it to the students and check to be sure that they understand the vocabulary and key concepts. At this point, it is not necessary to introduce the unit topics in any depth, since the unit preview activities that follow will achieve this goal.

Previewing the unit

Following the unit title page is a two-page spread that includes, on the right-hand side, a contents page listing the titles of the two chapters in the unit and the titles of the four sections in each chapter. Again, this unit contents page resembles the typical chapter or unit contents page of a university textbook. On the left-hand page of the spread are tasks that relate to the titles on the unit contents page. These tasks preview the unit either by having students predict what information might be found in each section or by giving them some information from the unit and having them respond to it. In this way, students are given an overview of the unit before they start reading it, to generate interest in the content of the unit. Furthermore, students are taught an important reading strategy, which is to preview the titles and headings of long readings.

Most of the activities in the unit preview are supposed to be done as pair work, followed by a report back to the whole class. The unit preview activities should take about one contact hour of class time to complete.

The readings

Each unit is divided into two chapters, and each chapter contains four readings. Each reading forms the basis for a lesson, which should take approximately two contact hours to teach. There are three stages to the lesson, corresponding to the three headings on the task pages. First, students do a number of prereading tasks under the heading "Preparing to Read." Then students read the text, following the instruction under the heading "Now Read." Finally, students carry out a number of postreading tasks to be found under the heading "After You Read."

Preparing to Read

In *Academic Encounters*, prereading is regarded as a crucial step in the reading process. Thus, before students embark on reading any section of the book, they are required to do a page of prereading tasks, found on the left-hand page facing the first page of the reading.

Prereading activities serve three main functions:
1 They familiarize students with the content of the reading, arousing their interest and activating any knowledge that they may already have on the topic.
2 They introduce students to reading attack strategies, giving students tools to be used when they undertake any future reading assignments.
3 They expose students to some of the language in the text, making the text easier to process when students actually do the reading.

Each page of prereading tasks should take approximately 20 minutes of class time. Of course, some may require more or less time.

Although one or two prereading tasks are always included before each reading, you should look for ways to supplement these tasks with additional prereading activities. As you and your students work through the book, students become exposed to more and more prereading strategies. Having been introduced to these, students should be adding them to their repertoire, and you should encourage their regular use. For example, after having practiced the prereading strategies of examining graphic material, previewing headings, and skimming, students should ideally carry out these operations before each and every reading.

In general, the lower the level of the students' reading and overall language proficiency, the more important extensive prereading becomes. The more prereading tasks that are done, the easier it becomes for students to access the text when it comes time for them to do a close reading.

Now Read

At the bottom of each "Preparing to Read" page is an instruction that tells the student to read the text. This is a deceptively simple instruction that begs an important question: How closely should the students read the text at this point? Some students, after doing prereading tasks such as skimming, believe that now they should read very slowly and carefully. But students should be discouraged from doing this. For one thing, it is a poor use of class time to have students poring silently over a text for 20 minutes or more, and more importantly it is vital that students at this level train themselves to read quickly, tolerating some ambiguity and going for understanding main ideas and overall text structure rather than every word and every detail.

To promote faster reading, each unit of the book contains one speed reading task, in which students time themselves and try to put into operation some techniques for faster reading. If students consistently apply these techniques, most texts will take between 3 and 7 minutes to read. Before students start reading any text, therefore, it is a good idea to give them a challenging time limit, within which they should aim to complete their reading of the text.

An alternative to doing every reading in class is to assign some of the longer readings as homework. When this is done, you should do the prereading task in class at the end of the lesson and then start the next class by having students quickly skim the text before moving on to the "After You Read" tasks.

After You Read

Often, after having completed a text reading, the first order of business is not to move on to the "After You Read" tasks, but to revisit the "Preparing to Read" tasks to check to see if students had the correct answers in a predicting or skimming activity, for example.

Like the "Preparing to Read" tasks, the "After You Read" tasks are of many different types and serve several different functions. You should not expect to find many conventional reading comprehension tasks. Instead students are often asked to demonstrate their understanding of a text in less direct ways, by doing language focus, study skill, and test preparation tasks, for each text in *Academic Encounters* is intended as an opportunity to develop a skill, not simply test comprehension.

Postreading tasks serve the following main functions:
1 They develop students' study skills repertoire by teaching them, for example, how to highlight a text, take notes in the margin or in notebooks, or guess the meaning of words in context.
2 They develop students' test preparation skills, asking them to assess what they would need to do if they were going to be tested on this text.
3 They ask students to think about the content, to find a personal connection to it perhaps, or apply new information in some way.

4 They highlight some of the most salient language in the text, either vocabulary or grammatical structures, and have students use that language in some way.

5 They have students read for meaning, look for main ideas, think critically about the text, or look for inferences.

6 They present students with a variety of different writing tasks, some of which may develop such key skills as summarizing and paraphrasing, others of which ask students to respond personally to the content of the reading in some way.

Because the "After You Read" tasks do not always deal in detail with reading comprehension or language issues, some teachers feel a sense of incompletion after coming to the end of an "After You Read" section. In this case, before moving on to another section of the chapter, it is worth going back over the text, reading the text to the students or along with the students, and picking out pieces of language that are worth drawing attention to and concepts that may have been overlooked.

The chapter writing assignments

Should you want your students to produce a longer piece of writing on the content of a chapter, each chapter ends with a choice of three writing assignment topics. You are free to adopt any methodology you wish in having students write on these topics. No methodology is recommended in this book, although most contemporary writing teachers would probably espouse a multi-draft approach with feedback on content for the early drafts and feedback on language and writing mechanics for later drafts.

The content quizzes

At the back of this teacher's manual are five content quizzes, one for each unit. These are not mentioned anywhere in the student's book. The purpose of giving the students quizzes is to simulate closely what might happen in a college course. In college, students do not just read a text one day and never have to think about it again. Instead, they are expected to read, remember what they have read, and be able to demonstrate their understanding of a text under test conditions. The content quizzes provide these conditions. Furthermore, the quizzes force the students to revisit the texts and apply the reading and test preparation strategies taught in the book. The quizzes also give students practice in answering different types of test questions, since each quiz contains a mixture of true/false, multiple choice, short answer, and short essay exam questions. Each quiz should take about 50 minutes of class time to complete, and the total score for each one is 50 points.

UNIT 1
Mind, Body, and Health

UNIT TITLE PAGE

Make sure students understand the three content words in the title. Elicit the adjectives associated with these words: *mental*, *physical*, and *healthy*. Contrast the terms *mental health* and *physical health*. Check to be sure that students know the phrases *to be in good/bad health* and *to be (un)healthy*.

Look at the picture. Ask students to tell you what the woman is doing. Ask if the students ever do yoga or something similar. Then have them describe the typical benefits of such exercises.

Read the unit summary paragraph with the students, checking to be sure that they understand the key concepts.

PREVIEWING THE UNIT

Draw students' attention to the task commentary box. Stress the importance of surveying unit and chapter titles and text headings and subheadings.

Chapter 1: The influence of mind over body

1➤ Before students do this step, introduce them to the phrases *to be under a lot of stress* or *to be under a great deal of stress*, *a stressful life/day/situation, job*. Students are often amused to learn the highly idiomatic expression *to be stressed out*.

2➤ In this step, students should do the true/false questions individually and then compare their answers. You can do one of the three things at this point: (1) reveal the correct answers, (2) tell the students to wait and find out the answers later when they study the text, (3) have students look quickly at the opening sentences only of paragraphs 1, 2, and 3 on page 19, which should give them enough information to be able to check their predicted answers.

Answers

_F_ 1   _F_ 2   _T_ 3

Chapter 2: Preventing illness

If you are planning to teach the units in order, these preview activities will most likely take place during the first class. Thus, the preview activities for Chapter 2 will give students the opportunity to interview and get to know a couple of classmates. During the interviews they will also learn something about their classmates' leisure activities and healthy and unhealthy habits. It is most important that steps 1 and 2 be performed with different partners. If not, students will hear more or less the same information, and they will be denied the opportunity of meeting another student in the class.

CHAPTER 1

The Influence of Mind Over Body

1 WHAT IS STRESS?

PREPARING TO READ

Thinking about the topic

1▶ Before students attempt to rate the different events according to the amount of stress they might cause, clarify each of the items in the list. Draw students' attention to the number of seemingly positive events listed – getting married, going on vacation, gaining a new family member. Ask them if they agree that these events can be viewed as stressful.

This step should be done by students individually. Make sure students put their initial rating in the column marked *Rank* and leave the column marked *Value* blank. Comparing answers can be done effectively as a pair or small group activity.

2▶ Before students assign values to events, you may need to give them an example of how this is done. For example, tell them that they might rate being fired from work as fairly stressful and give it a 63, and based on this they might rate changing to a new school as a 54, since it is also fairly stressful, but less so than being fired.

3▶ It is probably best for students to compare their answers with those in Figure A as a whole class activity. Students need to scan the whole chart to find the values.

4▶ Before attempting this step, which can be done as either a group work activity or a whole class activity, the teacher may need to clarify some of the items in Figure A on page 9 of the student book.

AFTER YOU READ

Task 1 Highlighting

If possible, have students bring different colored highlighter pens to this class. If students do not bring highlighter pens, have them underline and/or draw slash marks between the different parts of the text that they are asked to find. Ask students to acquire highlighter pens in the future, since other tasks in the book require them to be used.

1➤ This task is very straightforward. Draw students' attention to how some key terms are in bold print and some are in italics. Ask them which seem to be more important and why. Students should note that bold print is more noticeable than italics and that the terms in bold are also printed again in the margin together with a brief definition.

2, 3➤ Another way to do these steps is item by item, with students finding each definition or description, highlighting it, and then immediately comparing answers. You then confirm the correct answer.

Bring in a photocopy of the reading or a transparency of the reading and project on an overhead projector. Highlight the answers in different colors to demonstrate how effective highlighting can be.

Answers

- stress – emotional and physical reactions; stressors – stimuli or events in our environment that make physical and emotional demands on us
- they interfere with or threaten our accustomed way of life
- the organism becomes highly alert and aroused
- the organism tries to adapt to the stressful stimulus or to escape from it
- Whether a particular stimulus will be stressful depends on the person's subjective appraisal of that stimulus.

Task 2 Building vocabulary: Guessing meaning from context

Emphasize the importance of developing this skill, especially the idea of being satisfied with gaining a general idea of the meaning of unknown words – not having to know precise meanings. Illustrate this using the first paragraph of text. Students don't need to know exactly what a hurricane or a tornado is – all they need to understand is that they are types of disasters.

Also very important is the concept of looking for clues before and after the item in question. Have students look at the expression *daily hassles*, which appears in the first paragraph of text. Show them how, in order to get an idea of the meaning of this phrase, students need to look back – it is being contrasted with *major life events* (which *hassles* are not) – and forward to *having to wait in line in a supermarket* (which exemplifies the term). So a *daily hassle* is a small inconvenient problem that may happen to us during a typical day.

Have students try to work out the meanings of some of the other words themselves. Students should share their answers with the whole class and expound upon the line of reasoning that made them arrive at that particular meaning.

Task 3 Test-taking: Preparing for a short-answer quiz

Ask students if they have ever prepared for a quiz by trying to anticipate a professor's questions, which they then try to answer before the test. Go over the different question types in the task commentary box. While students write down questions, monitor their efforts and give suggestions for improvement.

When students ask each other their questions, note that the answers are to be given orally.

Task 4 Test-taking: Writing short answers to test questions

1► Students should be limited to about five minutes. Since they have already practiced orally the answers to these questions, it should not be difficult for the students to know what to put in their answers. The main idea is for students to get used to the idea of writing an exam answer in English quickly under time pressure, which they may never have had to do before.

2► After students compare answers with their partners, have the whole class listen to some of the questions and the answers. Alternatively, you might want to collect the answers and grade them.

2 STRESS AND ILLNESS

PREPARING TO READ

Building vocabulary: Synonyms and antonyms

Make sure that students understand the terms *synonym* and *antonym*. Have students do the activity individually. If they are unsure of the meaning of a word or phrase, have them scan the text for it so that the context may help them.

Answers

Synonyms (These answers do not need to be in the order given below.)

1 a disease   is similar in meaning to   an illness
2 to be anxious   is similar in meaning to   to be depressed
3 pressure   is similar in meaning to   stress
4 a pain   is similar in meaning to   an ache
5 to suffer from   is similar in meaning to   to be afflicted with

Antonyms (These answers do not need to be in the order given below.)

6 helpful   is nearly opposite in meaning to   harmful
7 to be sick   is nearly opposite in meaning to   to be well

Scanning

Answers

- common cold, cancer, arthritis, asthma, migraine headaches, ulcers
- assembly-line workers, air-traffic controllers
- eat too much or too little, sleep badly, smoke, drink, fail to exercise

AFTER YOU READ

Task 1 Language focus: Paraphrasing causality

Although this task is described as a language focus activity, it is equally a skill development task. The major emphasis of this task should be on developing the important skill of paraphrasing.

Have students scan the text for the cause and effect language of the table. Draw attention to the note at the bottom of the table, since many of the examples in the text use tentative language. Substitute some of the Xs and Ys in the table with sample sentences of your own.

1▶ Have students write their answers in class. Monitor their writing and suggest improvements. Have a whole-class sharing of the better answers.

2▶ In this step, students have to perform two things. First, they have to write the sentence from the text in note form, using an arrow to show the causal relation. (For some of the items this is quite tricky.) After having done that, they should write their paraphrase sentences.

Sample answers

1▶ *2* When people experience a great deal of stress, their stomachs may secrete too much hydrochloric acid, and as a result, they may get ulcers.
3 A great deal of stress can lead to mood changes in an individual, which may lead to depression, which may lead to too much drinking and smoking, thus causing illness.
4 When people experience a great deal of stress, they may pay more attention to their bodily reactions, which may lead them to decide that they are sick.

2▶ (Individual paraphrases of these notes will vary.)
2 great deal of job pressure ➤ different diseases
3 jobs with heavy psychological demands ➤ ulcers
4 stress ➤ mood and behavior changes ➤ disease

Task 2 Summarizing

Point out the difference between writing a summary and writing a paraphrase. Emphasize to the students the importance of practicing summary writing.

Answers

1▶ 2 *a*
5 *b*
1 *c*
6 *d*
4 *e*
3 *f*

2➤ Researchers have found that people who experience a great deal of stress in their daily lives or in their jobs are more likely to get sick. Stress, it seems, can cause the immune system not to function well and can cause harmful reactions such as an increase in acidic secretions in the stomach. Stress may also indirectly affect your health, since people who are under stress often engage in activities that are harmful.

---

3 COPING WITH STRESS

PREPARING TO READ

Predicting the content

Make sure students realize that each of the situations in 1–5 is described in the text and the answer to each of the questions is given in the text. It is probably a good idea to go through each situation with the whole class first, making sure that they understand all the vocabulary. At this point, have students decide individually whether they think answer *a* or *b* is the correct answer in each case. Then put students in pairs or small groups to compare answers and to explain why they think their answers are correct.

The pairs or groups should then compare their predictions with the whole class. Do not state what the correct answers to each situation will be at this point. Let the students discover them by reading the text. Since this is a fairly long reading, you might want to give the reading as homework and do the "After You Read" tasks the following day.

Answers

1 b
2 b
3 b
4 a
5 a

AFTER YOU READ

Task 1 Reading for main ideas

Remind students that the most important task in reading a text is to be able to understand the main ideas. Very detailed understanding is rarely necessary.

Answers

_c_	1
_a_	2
_b_	3
_b_	4
_b_	5

Task 2 Building vocabulary: Dealing with unknown words

1➤ Before students move on to step 2, have them tell you the different strategies they and their partners have come up with.

Sample answers

- Ignore the word. You can understand the main ideas of the text without knowing the meaning of this word or phrase.
- Ask the teacher to tell you its meaning.
- Record the word and later ask a native speaker of English to tell you its meaning.
- Look it up in the dictionary, especially if it seems to be important.
- Use the context to guess the meaning of the word.
- Look at the different parts of the word and see if you can work out its meaning from its parts.

Task 3 Writing a summary

Remind students how to construct a summary. You could have the students write the summary as a homework task. Alternatively, have students do a first draft in class, give them feedback, and then have them write a second draft as homework.

4 PSYCHOLOGY AND CANCER

PREPARING TO READ

Since this is one of the longer texts, you might want to do the "Preparing to Read" activities in class and then assign the reading as homework.

How much do you already know?

Questions 1 and 2 might make a good "mingle activity" in which students walk around the class, asking different students to tell them one body part that might be infected with cancer and one cancer-causing agent.

Questions 3, 4, and 5 are probably best done as a teacher-led activity, in which the teacher elicits as much information as possible from the whole class.

Building vocabulary: Learning word clusters

You might want to introduce the concept of making semantic maps as a way of collecting topic vocabulary. In a semantic map a central term such as *cancer* is placed at the center of a network of related words radiating out from it, each one connected to a different node of the network.

It is suggested that this activity be done as pair work. Have students quickly share their ideas about the meanings of the words in bold. Then go over the words with the whole class.

AFTER YOU READ

Task 1 Scanning

Students should do this task individually. When finished, draw attention to the convention used for citing studies, in which the date of the study (or its publication) is given in parentheses after the name or names of the researchers who wrote up the study, and *et al.* is used to represent the names of all authors after the first named author for studies involving more than two authors.

Answers

6	a
5	b
5	c
3	d
6	e
3, 7	f

Task 2 Reading for detail

Point out how the arrows are used to indicate causation. Students should work individually to find the answers and then compare them.

Answers

b	1
f	2
d	3
e	4
c	5
a	6

Task 3 Citing studies in your writing

Explain the concept of *citation*. Contrast this with *quotation*. Put on the board the formulaic sentence pattern given in the task commentary box. Explain what is supposed to fit into each part of the formula. Go over the sample sentence on the bottom of page 22 in the student book.

Have students try to do the first item individually. Point out the similarity between doing this exercise and the paraphrasing exercises on pages 12 and 13. Student answers may be put on the board and analyzed.

At the end of Section 4, you might want to refer your students back to the questions that were answered in the "Preparing to Read" task: How much do you already know?

Sample answers

1 In a study of women with cancer, Greer and Morris (1981) found that women who showed a fighting spirit had a better chance of recovering from the disease.

2 In a study of helplessness in animals, Laudenslager et al. (1979) found that animals faced with a stress they could not escape had fewer lymphocytes in their blood.

3 In a study of the relationship between depression and cancer, Shekelle (1981) found that men who were diagnosed with depression had a greatly increased chance of dying of cancer.

4 In a study of mice injected with cancer cells, Sklar and Anisman (1979) found that there was a relationship between how helpless the mice were and the speed at which their cancers grew.

5 In a study of women with breast cancer, Levy (1984) found that those women who expressed anger at having the disease had a better chance of recovering than women who did not.

CHAPTER 1 Writing assignment

Go over the questions, eliciting from students which text or texts might be helpful to review in answering each one. Put students who are going to answer the same question in pairs to brainstorm how they might answer it.

CHAPTER 2

Preventing Illness

1 HEART DISEASE

PREPARING TO READ

Personalizing the topic

Discuss the assertion in the task commentary box. Point out to students that personalization should also occur after reading, when one tries to apply new information to one's own life and situation.

Explain the concept of being at risk for heart disease. Go through the questionnaire item by item, explaining where necessary, while the students check yes or no. Without revealing the answer (which is that the highest risk person is someone who answers yes to all seven questions), ask students to predict what they think would be the highest risk set of answers.

Remember that after reading the text students should look back at the questionnaire to see which set of answers represented the highest risk for heart disease. Find out from the students, in a lighthearted way, who is most at risk and who is least at risk.

Skimming for main ideas

Spend time explaining what skimming involves and why it is such an important skill to practice.

Answers

2	a
6	b
3	c
1	d
4	e
5	f

AFTER YOU READ

Task 1 Test-taking: Answering true/false questions about a text

Go over the list of strategies for answering true/false questions given in the task commentary box. Then have students answer the questions individually, referring back to the text to find their answers. When finished, have students compare answers in pairs, showing each other the places in the text which justify their answers.

Go over the correct answers as a whole class activity. Ask students to justify their answers. Where appropriate, refer back to the strategies listed to see if they help in deciding if an answer is true or false. For example, the opening part of the statement in question 6 is true, but the next part of the statement is false, making the whole statement false.

Answers

F	1
T	2
T	3
T	4
F	5
F	6
F	7
T	8
F	9
T	10

Task 2 Language focus: Making comparisons

This mini grammar lesson is almost certainly going to be a review for students at this level, thus in one page a lot of ground is quickly covered. Come to class with some sample adjectives to illustrate how the number of syllables–one, two, three, or more–can affect how the comparative adjective is formed.

Steps 1 and 2 can be written in class. Alternatively, some of the items can be done in class and the rest written for homework.

Task 3 Writing a paragraph

The topic of Type A and Type B personalities is an excellent one for writing a compare-and-contrast paragraph. Before having students write, teachers might review some of the ways in which one can compare and contrast in English, using transitional expressions such as *while, although, on the other hand*, and so on.

This paragraph could make a good homework assignment. Teachers could help students develop the structure of the paragraph in class by helping them formulate a topic sentence and think through the details that they want to include.

2 SMOKING

PREPARING TO READ

Thinking about the topic

Students should work with a partner. After students discuss the two questions on each topic with a partner, have them share their answers with the class.

Skimming for main ideas

Review how to skim before students begin this task. Hurry the students along, making sure they skim, not read.

Answers

3	*a*
6	*b*
1	*c*
5	*d*
4	*e*
2	*f*

AFTER YOU READ

Task 1 Analyzing paragraph organization

Explain to the students what a "listing paragraph" is. You may wish to give the students some simple examples of opening statements of listing paragraphs, such as, "There are many different kinds of whales," and "There are two kinds of elephants."

Make sure that students know what an outline is and then have them complete the partial outlines. Monitor students as they do their outlines. Have them compare answers with a partner and then share their answers with the whole class.

Answers

Paragraph 2: Reasons why people start and cannot stop smoking

    a reasons for starting: peer pressure

    b reason cannot stop 1: *physiological addiction*

    c reason cannot stop 2: *psychological addiction*

Paragraph 3: *Smoking cessation programs*

    a technique 1: *aversive conditioning*

    b technique 2: stimulus control

Paragraph 5: Smoking prevention programs

    a program type 1:   explanation of risks

    b program type 2: *role-play resisting offers*

Task 2 Writing a listing paragraph

Before students write one of the paragraphs from their completed outlines, remind them how to paraphrase, using their own words only. These short paragraphs are best done by writing a first draft in class, receiving some teacher feedback, and then writing a second draft for homework.

Task 3 Dramatizing the text

A role play can provide a way to make vivid a concept within a text, and it can also provide an unusual and interesting mode for students to demonstrate their understanding of what they read. Always make sure students have sufficient time to prepare the role play.

Instead of having all students act out their role plays in front of the class (which would soon become boring), consider having all the students doing the first role play act out their role plays simultaneously while being observed by the students doing the second role play, then vice versa. Have one or two of the role plays performed in front of the whole class.

Task 4 Language focus: Awareness of levels of formality

The main purpose of this brief activity is to draw the students' attention to the concept of register. You might want to discuss briefly the differences between written and spoken English as a lead-in to a discussion about when formal and informal styles of writing or speaking are and are not appropriate.

Answers

1 *quit*
2 *to get hooked*
3 *the weed*
4 *quitters*
5 *the knack*

---

3 EXERCISE

PREPARING TO READ

Thinking about the topic

Students should work briefly in pairs and then report to the whole class.

Speed reading

Stress how important it is that students develop the habit of reading quickly when doing academic work. Carefully explain each of the items in the list of "Techniques for Speed Reading" found in the task commentary box. Have students practice these techniques as they read the text.

AFTER YOU READ

Task 1 Reading for detail

As soon as students have read quickly through the text, they should write down their time and then answer the reading comprehension questions without looking back at the text. Go around the class, looking at students' answers. Tell them which ones they got right and which ones are wrong.

Answers

1 a
2 b
3 c
4 a
5 b
6 b
7 c
8 c
9 a
10 c

Follow-up: How well did you read?

Help students complete the box and calculate their words per minute rate and percent correct. (You may want to bring a calculator to class.)

Task 2 Writing a summary

Consider having students do this as a homework assignment.

4 WELLNESS

PREPARING TO READ

Thinking about the topic

1➤ Give students some ideas to get them started on their list. Encourage them to write short items, such as, "Get 8 hours sleep a night" or "Eat a low-fat diet." Remind them that they can choose negative items, such as, "Do not smoke."

2➤ In this step, students must reach a group consensus as to the best six items in all their lists.

4➤ In this step, you will probably want to write each group's items on the board so that the class can then vote for the six most important items.

5➤ At the end of the activity it is amusing to find out who is the healthiest person in the class, that is, who does all or most of the six items on the list. You could also find out who is the least healthy person in the class, provided it is done in a lighthearted manner.

AFTER YOU READ

Asking clarification questions about a text

1➤ Before students read the text, explain the task to be done after reading. Read through the five questions in step 1, so that students are exposed to the problem parts of the text before they read.

2➤ The answers to the five questions are not easy. Instead of having students work in pairs for step 2, it may be best if you role-play the discussion leader, with different students asking you the questions. Perhaps as a follow-up, students could then pair up to do the same mini role play.

CHAPTER 2 Writing assignment

Go over the questions, eliciting from students which text or texts might be helpful to review in answering each one. Put students who are going to answer the same question in pairs to brainstorm how they might answer it.

UNIT 2
Development Through Life

UNIT TITLE PAGE

One way to introduce this unit is to elicit the following vocabulary items: *baby, infant, child, boy, girl, kid, adult, man, woman.* You could place these words in a chart on the board with columns for "male," "female," and "either male or female." The rows going down could go from younger to older. Then introduce some terms relating to periods of life: *infancy, childhood, adolescence,* and *adulthood.*

Go over the unit summary paragraph at the bottom of the page. Check to be sure that students understand the main concepts.

PREVIEWING THE UNIT

Remind students that this activity will give them an overview of what they are going to read about and study, and that previewing the titles on a contents page is a useful activity when studying from textbooks in a college course.

Have students work in pairs. After each step, stop and have a whole-class sharing of ideas.

Chapter 3: Adolescence

Sample answers

1▶ *1* Going to secondary school, sexually developing so that you are capable of having children, being able to look after yourself at home alone, etc.
2 Leaving high school, leaving college, getting a job, leaving home, etc.
3 There is no correct answer but the typical range given is 12 to 19 years old.

2▶ Failing an examination, losing a girlfriend or boyfriend, having trouble at school, being depressed for no reason, etc.

Chapter 4: Adulthood

Sample answers

1▶ *1* Early adulthood: getting married, having a baby, moving into a new house, finding a job, etc. Middle adulthood: having more responsibility at work, dealing with the death of one's parents, helping one's children get through adolescence, etc.
2 Early adulthood: from <u>20</u> to <u>40</u> years old
   Middle adulthood: from <u>41</u> to <u>65</u> years old

2▶ Retirement, children gone from home, illness, death of spouse, etc.

Chapter 3

Adolescence

Have students look at the picture that opens Chapter 3. Ask them if any young people in their countries look like this. No doubt this picture will date quickly, so ask students to tell you how rebellious teens look and act today in their countries and in any other countries that they know about.

1 Defining Adolescence

PREPARING TO READ

Personalizing the topic

Make sure students understand the concept of a stereotype. Look at the cartoon at the bottom of the page and ask students to describe it in detail. Ask students if teenage kids ever talk to their parents in this manner in their country. What would happen if they did?

Go over the items in the questionnaire, making sure that students understand each item. After students respond to the questions, they can compare answers with a partner and then report to the whole class. In a lighthearted way, find out which student had the most difficult adolescence, i.e., circled the lowest numbers, and who had the least difficult, i.e., circled the highest numbers. Include yourself in the discussion. Tell your students how you scored.

Before reading the text, have students look at the pictures and the marginal notes to get an overview of the text. Also have them look at Task 1, "Reading for the Main Idea," and read the three choices for the main idea of the text. This will provide a focus for their reading.

AFTER YOU READ

Task 1 Reading for the main idea

Answer

1 There are three different ways to define adolescence.

Task 2 Analyzing paragraph organization

The purpose of this activity is to make students aware of how certain words in a text may refer backwards or forwards to previously mentioned and yet-to-be mentioned ideas in the text.

1➤ While students are looking at the skeleton paragraph, read the second paragraph of the text to them. As you read, call out the number of each sentence indicating where each sentence begins and ends. Draw attention to the words and phrases in the skeleton. Do this before students answer the questions.

Let students work alone on questions 1–4. Monitor students to see if they are able to do the tasks.

Answers

1a Sentences one and two
1b Sentences three and four
1c Sentences five, six, and seven

2a Or
2b Additionally

(Wording for 3a–c will vary.)
3a When adolescence is viewed in biological terms
3b When adolescence is viewed from a psychological perspective
3c Looking at adolescence as a social stage

4 There is no topic sentence. Two possible topic sentences might be: "There are three ways to define adolescence," or "Adolescence may be viewed from three very different perspectives."

2➤ When students have answered all the questions, let them compare answers with a partner.

2 PHYSICAL CHANGE IN ADOLESCENCE

PREPARING TO READ

Examining graphic material

There are a number of steps that students should be encouraged to go through every time they approach a new text to be read. These include looking at headings, looking for words in bold and italics in the text, looking at the graphic material, and skimming. In this task, students are asked to look at the graphic material. Help students create a list of all the different types of graphic material that may be in a text.

Students should look at Figure 3.1 in the text, and answer the question individually. Students should then compare answers.

Answers

(Wording will vary.)

1 Girls start their growth spurt earlier than boys.
2 Girls stop growing earlier than boys.
3 Boys gain more height during their growth spurts than girls.

Skimming for main ideas

◢ *Answers*

1➤   <u>4</u> *a*
  <u>5</u> *b*
  <u>3</u> *c*
  <u>2</u> *d*

AFTER YOU READ

Task 1 Reading for detail

Have students answer the question individually. Then have them compare answers in pairs, showing each other the places in the text that support their answers. Then students can share their answers with the whole class.

◢ *Answers*

  <u>2</u> *a* An early-maturing girl has many advantages.
  <u>3</u> *b* A late-maturing girl does not suffer as many disadvantages as a late maturing boy.
  <u>1</u> *c* Best is to be an early-maturing male. (end of paragraph 5)
  <u>4</u> *d* Worst is to be a late-maturing boy.

The answer above may depend on whether one is judging from the point of view of the adolescent at the time of his or her adolescence or from some later point in time. Early-maturing girls have advantages over late-maturing girls at the time of their adolescence. However, from the perspective of later life, i.e., adulthood, the text tells us that it may be better to have been a late-maturing girl (see the middle of paragraph 5).

Task 2 Language focus: Gerunds as subjects

It is sometimes difficult for a student to untangle a sentence that has a long subject. It is particularly difficult when the long subject is a verb phrase. This task draws students' attention to such instances and has them practice making some simple sentences with gerunds as subjects.

  Make sure students understand what a gerund is before they do the exercise. Point out how gerunds are more commonly the objects of certain verbs than the subjects, e.g. "She enjoys dancing," or "He finished eating."

◢ *Answers*

1➤ • Reaching puberty well before or well after others of one's age *(subject)* does have *(verb)*
  • Being a late bloomer *(subject)* is *(verb)*
  • Being a late bloomer *(subject)* was *(verb)*

◢ *Sample answers*

2➤ *1* Being a late bloomer <u>*can have many disadvantages*</u> for a boy.
  2 Reaching puberty early <u>*is often an advantage*</u> for a girl.

3 Maturing late <u>*is not always a disadvantage*</u> for a girl.
4 Being an early bloomer <u>*can have a very positive affect on self-esteem*</u> for a boy.

Task 3 Personalizing the topic

Students should discuss the questions in pairs and later report their answers to the whole class.

---

3 COGNITIVE AND SOCIAL DEVELOPMENT IN ADOLESCENCE

PREPARING TO READ

The SQR3 System (Part I)

This is one of the longer texts in the book, so teachers might want to do the "Preparing to Read" task in class and have students read the text more closely at home.

Tell students that you are going to teach them a system of study skills that is often taught to North American high school and college students. Even if students do not want to adopt the system in its entirety, they should find it useful to know about, since there may be elements that they will want to incorporate into their own study skills system.

Students should survey the text, formulate questions from headings and subheadings, and read the text with their questions in mind.

AFTER YOU READ

Task 1 Note-taking in the margins

It is assumed that students will already have some knowledge about note-taking. If they do not, teachers may need to spend some time on the conventional abbreviations and symbols used in note-taking.

1➤ Have students discuss these questions about note-taking with a partner.

2➤ Students should analyze the sample notes for the section "Identity Formation."

3➤ Have students insert sample notes for the section "Adolescent Egocentrism" as directed.

4➤ Finally, students create their own notes for the section "The Influence of Family," and compare their notes with a partner.

Task 2 The SQR3 System (Part II)

1➤ At this point, students should have marginal notes for each of the three sections of the text. Students should read one of those sections and then give an oral summary to a partner. They can use their marginal notes to help them.

2> To save time in class, teachers might want students to do the final stage of the SQR3 system, "Review," as a homework assignment.

Task 3 Personalizing the topic

These questions probably are best addressed in a whole class discussion, although pair work is also possible.

Task 4 Writing a summary

The task commentary box provides an important and oft-overlooked rationale for writing summaries of a text. Review it with the students before they write. Also remind students to use their own words in a summary, as always.

---

4 TEENAGE SUICIDE

PREPARING TO READ

Predicting the content

Explain this task carefully. Students should predict a rank order. Have students tell you their predictions, but don't give them the correct answers. Have them check their answers after they do the reading.

Answers

Rank	Cause of death
1	accidents
2	murder
3	suicide
4	disease (This is to be inferred.)

Skimming for main ideas

When skimming, students do not have to read the information in Figure 3.2 in the text. This will be looked at separately in Task 2 in the "After You Read" part of Section 4.

Answers

  2 a

  3 b

  1 c

AFTER YOU READ

Task 1 Reading for detail

Answers

1 b

2 c

3 (Wording will vary.)

   (1) *know that teenage suicide is a real problem*

   (2) *bring discussion of suicide into the open*

   (3) *learn the signs of impending suicide*

   (4) *peers must be educated to be good listeners*

   (5) *peers must be able to suggest therapy for friends contemplating suicide*

Task 2 Applying what you know: Analyzing new data

Mention the popularity of case studies in academic course work. Discuss why case studies are useful. Go over the information in Figure 3.2 with the class, clarifying any vocabulary or difficult concepts. Give students enough time to read about the four teenagers and to make a decision as to who they think is the most and who the least likely to commit suicide. Then put students in groups and have them defend their choices. They should support their arguments by referring to the information in Figure 3.2.

CHAPTER 3 Writing assignment

Go over the questions, eliciting from students which text or texts might be helpful to review in answering each one. Put students who are going to answer the same question in pairs to brainstorm how they might answer it.

CHAPTER 4

Adulthood

Ask students to remember what they said in the unit preview about when adolescence ends and when adulthood begins. Have students look at the picture on page 71 of the student book. Where are these people gathered? Why do students think this picture is being used to illustrate the chapter on adulthood?

1 EARLY ADULTHOOD

PREPARING TO READ

Personalizing the topic

Students should check the questions they have been faced with. Ask around the class about who checked which items. If you feel comfortable doing so, reveal to students which items you would have checked.

Building vocabulary: Collocations

Collocation is an important but neglected area of language. You may want to illustrate the concept with some simple examples. For example, put on the board, "to drive _____" and "to ride _____." Ask students which words might go in the blank spaces.

Point out to students how certain adjectives are more likely to occur with certain nouns. For example, you can say a "good," "great," or "excellent opportunity;" possibly you can say a "big opportunity," but certainly you would rarely if ever say a "large opportunity." Tell students to be aware of which words go together and to record collocations in their notebooks when learning new words.

This exercise is more easily done if students work their way down the column of verbs, trying to find the matching collocating noun, rather than start with the nouns and try to find the collocating verbs. Students should work individually and then compare answers in pairs. Note that there are only nine verbs because *make* is used twice in the answers. When students share their answers in open class, accept more than one correct answer and then, before students read the text, reveal the collocations that actually occur in the text.

Answers

The verbs in parentheses are also acceptable, although they are not the verbs that collocate with these nouns in the text.

1	to pursue	a career *(follow)*
2	to seek	advice *(follow)*
3	to attain	adult status
4	to make	a decision
5	to take	responsibility
6	to earn	money *(raise, make)*
7	to raise	a family
8	to follow	a path *(seek, pursue)*
9	to make	a choice
10	to address	an issue *(raise)*

AFTER YOU READ

Task 1 Reading for detail

Point out to your students that these questions rely on their using their critical thinking skills. Have students work in pairs and then open the questions to the whole class.

Sample answers

1 By law, there are often different ages at which one can do the following: buy/drink alcohol, vote, buy/smoke cigarettes, get married, go to an adults-only movie, be sent to prison, etc.

2 Young adults become more independent (they no longer need parents to help make decisions); young adults also often become more dependent (they often establish a significant relationship with someone with whom they make joint decisions about the important issues in their lives).

3 Family life and career

4 On the one hand, many people want to earn as much as possible in their work; on the other, they want a job that is interesting and personally satisfying–these two forces may be in conflict. A further complicating factor may be what your parents or family want you to do professionally, which may not be what you want to do.

5 Young adulthood requires a great deal of energy. Fortunately, this is the time when we have most energy, otherwise we wouldn't be able to survive all the pressure put upon us.

Task 2 Personalizing the topic

Discuss and clarify each item before students check their choices. Have students compare their answers in pairs; then have some students read their choices to the whole class. Share with your students how you would have answered this question.

Task 3 Personal writing

Discuss with students the advantages of keeping a journal in English, and discuss the mechanics of how to do it. Students could then either write for ten minutes in class or do this assignment for homework.

2 MARRIAGE AND FAMILY

PREPARING TO READ

How much do you already know?

Ask students to answer the multiple-choice questions. Go over each answer, eliciting from the students their choices, without telling them what the correct answers are. As soon as they have finished reading the text, however, they should go back to their answers and see how many they predicted correctly.

Answers

1 b
2 c
3 a
4 a
5 b
6 c
7 a
8 b

AFTER YOU READ

Task 1 Language focus: Expressing confidence in the truth or accuracy of a fact

Explain to students that in academic work it is important to be able to make statements that assess the amount of evidence there is for a fact. This task helps students to make such statements.

1▶ Have students look at the two sentences taken from the text. Have them find a third similar sentence in the final paragraph of the text. ("There is no doubt that having a baby . . .")

2▶ Have students look at the chart. Discuss the difference between "there is" and "there seems to be." Note the different strengths of the quantifiers, "a great deal of," "some," etc. Note also how the sentence openers "there is little doubt that" and "there is a great deal of evidence that" are very similar in meaning.
   Have students add expressions from the chart to qualify statements 1–6, basing their choices on the information they find in the text. After writing their sentences, they should be able to go back to the text to justify their answers.

Sample answers

1 There seems to be little evidence to suggest that fewer Americans are choosing to get married.
2 There is some evidence to suggest that most Americans believe that having a successful marriage leads to a happy life.
3 There is little evidence to suggest that Americans tend to marry someone who is opposite to themselves in many ways.
4 There seems to be little doubt that it is difficult to have a successful marriage.

5 There is little evidence to suggest that, on the whole, men and women value very different qualities in a mate.

6 There is little doubt that women are more concerned than men about whether their spouse has good earning capacity.

Task 2 Personalizing the topic

Have students discuss questions 1 and 2 in groups and then report back their answers to the whole class. Then, before they attempt question 3, clarify each of the items in the bulleted list and have students rank order the items individually. Then put the students in groups again and instruct them to explain and justify their rank order. Ask each group to try to come to consensus with a rank ordering that all members of the group can agree to. Again, report back to the whole class before doing question 4.

   For question 4, give students time to write the three most and least important qualities they require in a mate, before they do the group work. Then they share their answers and explain their choices.

Task 3 Personal writing

Refer back to the rationale for personal writing in the task commentary box on page 73. Students can write for ten minutes in class or at home.

3 MIDDLE ADULTHOOD

PREPARING TO READ

Thinking about the topic

Remind students of the age ranges for middle adulthood that they came up with in "Previewing the Unit." Ask them to think of the physical changes that can occur in this period and write them down in short sentences. This activity could be done equally well in a class brainstorming session in which you write the sentences on the board.

Sample answers

Hair may begin to fall out or thin. Hair turns gray or white. The muscles lose their strength and flexibility. The stomach/waistline may get bigger. Women can no longer have babies. Knees may ache. People are more likely to get back problems. Teeth may fall out or turn yellow. People get lines on the face. People get shadows under the eyes. Skin loses its flexibility. Eyesight gets worse.

Building vocabulary: Guessing meaning from context

Remind students of the importance of this skill. Go over the answers in class.

AFTER YOU READ

Task 1 Reading for main ideas

Before students read the text, have them read the four sentences in this task.

Answers

_1_	a
_3_	b
_4_	c
_2_	d

Task 2 Applying what you read

Have students think about the title of this task. Reflect upon the importance of being able to apply the knowledge that one gains from studying and reading.

1➤ Give students a few minutes to think about a person they know who is in middle adulthood (this person could be themselves if they are old enough). Clarify each of the items in the box. At the same time, students can check the boxes that apply.

2➤ Students can make a short presentation to a partner or to the class about this person, indicating which challenges he or she has had to meet. If this is to be a presentation to the whole class, you might have students first give rehearsal presentations in pairs and then give their presentations to the whole group.

---

4 LATE ADULTHOOD

PREPARING TO READ

Thinking about the topic

Clarify the items in the questionnaire. Students should complete the questionnaire and then share their answers in pairs. When students reveal their answers in class, ask who rated an item as 1, 3, 5, etc. If students from the same country are in the class, see if they agree with their compatriots.

Speed reading

Review the speed-reading guidelines in the task commentary box on page 36 of the student book. If you have done a speed-reading exercise from a previous unit in the book, see if students can list the techniques without looking at page 36.

Before students start reading, make sure they know exactly what to do when they finish reading.

AFTER YOU READ

Task 1 Reading for detail

Students should read quickly, write down their time when finished, and then do the reading comprehension questions without looking back at the text. Go around the class, looking at students' answers. Tell students which ones they got right and which are wrong.

Answers

 1 a
 2 c
 3 b
 4 c
 5 a
 6 c
 7 b
 8 a
 9 b
10 b

Follow-up: How well did you read?

After going over the reading comprehension questions with the class, help students fill in the box in the follow-up activity. Bring a calculator to class to help work out students' word-per-minute rates.

Task 2 Reading critically

Go over the task commentary box. Stress how important it is that students develop the habit of reading critically. Students should discuss the myths in pairs, or this can be done as a whole class activity. Make sure reference is made back to the text, as well as to students' own experiences.

Task 3 Writing a summary

Remind students of the guidelines for writing a summary. (See the task commentary box on page 13 for a review.)

CHAPTER 4 Writing assignment

Go over the questions, eliciting from students which text or texts might be helpful to review in answering each one. Put students who are going to answer the same question in pairs to brainstorm how they might answer it.

UNIT 3
Intelligence

UNIT TITLE PAGE

Elicit from students some of the expressions used in English to describe people's intelligence. These will include adjectives ranging from *dumb* to *brilliant*, and nouns such as *idiot* and *genius*. Point out any connotations surrounding these words, such as which are offensive and which are formal or informal. Tell students the readings in this unit focus on why we describe some people as intelligent and others as unintelligent, and how people come to be one or the other.

Read the unit summary paragraph with the students, making sure they understand the main concepts.

PREVIEWING THE UNIT

Chapter 5: Assessing intelligence

Make sure students understand the title of Chapter 5.

1➤ Put students in pairs and have them discuss the three questions in step 1. Afterwards, call on pairs to report their discussion. Question 3 often makes for a very interesting cross-cultural discussion when students from many different nationalities are in the class.

2➤ Before students discuss these questions, make sure they understand what a stereotype is. You may prefer to do this step in a class brainstorming session, rather than have students discuss it in pairs first. A typical answer might be that the stereotypical brainy child is skinny, unathletic, has thick glasses, has difficulty making friends, etc. Point out that stereotypes are often inaccurate.

Chapter 6: Accounting for variations in intelligence

Make sure students understand the title of Chapter 6. The questions previewing this chapter are all predictive. Since students are usually eager to find out if they have correctly predicted something, it is probably best to reveal the answers to the questions immediately after hearing their predictions, rather than keeping the students in suspense and waiting till they have studied the chapter.

Answers

1➤ <u>False</u> *1*
   <u>True</u> *2*

2➤ *4* This will always be an impossible question to answer.

CHAPTER 5

Assessing Intelligence

1 INTELLIGENCE DEFINED

PREPARING TO READ

Thinking about the topic

Tell students that in the text they are going to read some definitions of intelligence, but first they are going to try to define intelligence themselves. Put students in pairs to brainstorm a list of the criteria by which they judge someone to be intelligent. Write those ideas on the board. See if there is agreement about what the main characteristics of an intelligent person are.

   Leave the list on the board so that when they have finished reading, students can compare their ideas with those in the text.

Sample answers

Intelligent people:

- have good memories
- know a lot about a lot of different things
- can answer questions more quickly than others
- can solve problems easily
- find interesting answers that other people don't think of
- do well on tests

Skimming for main ideas

Before doing this activity, students must understand the concept of an operational definition and its differences from a theoretical or commonsense definition. You can try to explain an operational definition by giving an example. For instance, if scientists want to study old people, they may define an old person as anyone over 65 years of age. Is that a good definition of being old? No, but it enables scientists to operate, i.e., study the problem without having to worry about a definitional issue for which there may be no precise answer.

Answers

_3_	a
_4_	b
_1_	c
_2_	d

AFTER YOU READ

Task 1 Reading for detail

In going over the answers to these questions, have the students go back to the text to find the precise wording that leads to the correct answers.

Answers

1 Three definitions are given: (1) it depends on the total amount of our knowledge – "the sum total of everything you know," (2) our ability to learn from experience, (3) our ability to solve problems

2 c

3 "that which intelligence tests measure"– in other words, you can be called intelligent if you get above a certain score on an intelligence test

Task 2 Building vocabulary: Collocations

Too often students look for new (unfamiliar) single words in a text and ignore how words they are familiar with collocate with other words. The purpose of this activity is to encourage students to look back through the text to find collocations.

Answers

1➤ to learn from *experience*   to present   *ambiguities*
    to solve   *problems*   to pose   *problems*
    to cope with   *challenges*   to overcome   *difficulties*

2➤
A	**B**
to attack a problem	to confront a problem
to face a problem	to tackle a problem
to solve a problem	to be posed with a problem
to have a problem	to overcome a problem

3➤ Imagine you *have/are posed with* a problem. It is no good running away from that problem. You must *face/confront* the problem and really *attack/tackle* it. Hopefully, in the end you will then *overcome/solve* your problem.

---

2 THE STANFORD-BINET INTELLIGENCE TEST

PREPARING TO READ

Examining graphic material

Preview all the types of graphic material that should be previewed before reading a text.

1➤ Tell students that the terms *crystallized abilities* and *fluid/analytic abilities* are technical terms in psychology and not part of everyday speech. To get students started on this activity and to help clarify the task, give one of the answers for verbal reasoning, quantitative reasoning, abstract/visual reasoning, and short-term memory. Show students where these answers should be written in Figure B.

Answers

2►

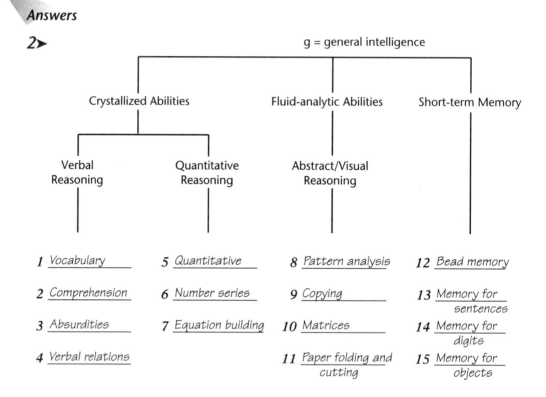

g = general intelligence

Crystallized Abilities   Fluid-analytic Abilities   Short-term Memory

Verbal   Quantitative   Abstract/Visual
Reasoning   Reasoning   Reasoning

1 Vocabulary   *5* Quantitative   *8* Pattern analysis   *12* Bead memory

2 Comprehension   *6* Number series   *9* Copying   *13* Memory for
                                                                                     sentences

3 Absurdities   *7* Equation building   *10* Matrices   *14* Memory for
                                                                                     digits

4 Verbal relations   *11* Paper folding and   *15* Memory for
                                                        cutting   objects

AFTER YOU READ

Task 1 Effective note-taking

If students have already done Task 1, "Note-taking in the Margins," on page 61, remind them about marginal notes and the relative advantages and disadvantages of marginal notes over notes on separate note paper.

In going over the guidelines in the task commentary box, clarify all the points with good examples. For instance, check that students know some of the conventional abbreviations and symbols used in note-taking. Show students on a piece of paper approximately how much margin to leave to the left and right of notes. Show on the board how indentation works.

1► Go over the sample notes for the first four paragraphs with the students, checking to be sure that they understand the abbreviations. Then put students in pairs to summarize the main points from the notes.

2, 3► You might want your students to do step 2 as homework, with step 3 being done in class on the day that the homework is due.

Task 2 Test-taking: Preparing for a short-answer quiz

1➤ Look back at the information about different types of test questions, displayed in the task commentary box in Task 3 on page 8. Then have students write four short-answer questions. Encourage them to write different types of questions. As students write, monitor for accurate question formation.

2➤ When students have finished writing, students should ask their questions in class. Have other students respond to these questions orally and let the rest of the class evaluate the accuracy and completeness of their answers.

---

3 THE WECHSLER INTELLIGENCE TESTS

PREPARING TO READ

Building background knowledge on the topic

In this prereading task, students are given some information about the Wechsler tests before they start reading. Draw students' attention to the task commentary box, which asserts that it is easier to process new information from a text when one already has some knowledge of the subject matter. Ask students how they might apply this advice in their own college reading. For example, before reading a chapter assignment, students could look up some dictionary or encyclopedic information on the topic of the reading.

Answers

Put the panels in a meaningful order = Picture arrangement
Put this puzzle together = Object assembly
Fill in the appropriate symbol = Digit symbol
Supply the missing feature = Picture completion
Copy the design, using another set of blocks = Block design

AFTER YOU READ

Task 1 Reading for detail

This is one of the few true/false exercises in the book. A useful sequence of procedures for doing such exercises in class is (1) have students answer the questions individually; (2) when finished, look at their answers and tell them how many they have wrong; (3) students try to find their wrong answers and correct them; (4) students compare answers with their partners; (5) teacher calls on students in class to read the statement and say if it is true or false; (6) teacher asks students to find evidence in the text to support their answers.

Answers

T	1
T	2
T	3
F	4
F	5
T	6
F	7
F	8

Task 2 Applying what you read: Designing a test

This task is best done as a project and may take several days to complete. Students are assigned to groups to create their own intelligence test, based on the descriptions of the subtests of the Wechsler verbal scale. Each student in the group might be given a different part of the test to design. The groups may need to meet outside class, and also some class time might be reserved for groups to meet and work on the project. If a word processor is available, students might want to type up their tests so that they have good quality copies when they give the test to other students.

4 GIFTEDNESS

PREPARING TO READ

Thinking about the topic

Before students look at the pictures, teach them the following set of vocabulary items that come up in the text: *to have a gift, talent, special ability, skill,* or *flair for doing something*.

As students look at the pictures, elicit what sort of special skills or gifts the young people in the pictures are exhibiting.

Speed reading

Always go over the guidelines for faster reading on page 36 of the student book before doing a speed reading task. Also check to be sure that students understand exactly what to do when they have finished reading. (See page 36 for details.)

AFTER YOU READ

Task 1 Reading for detail

Students should read quickly, write down their time when finished, and then answer the reading comprehension questions without looking back at the text. Go around the class, checking students' answers. Tell them which ones they got right and which wrong. After students correct their mistakes, have them report their answers to the whole class, indicating which part of the text supports their answers.

Answers

 1 a
 2 b
 3 b
 4 a
 5 b
 6 c
 7 c
 8 a
 9 c
10 b

Follow-up: How well did you read?

1► Help students complete the box and calculate their words-per-minute rate and percent correct.

Task 2 Personalizing the topic

2► Tell students that when they do step 2 they should give details to justify their answers. It is also worth teaching the following sentence frame to help students express themselves:

> "I'm terrible/hopeless/not very good/pretty good/really good at . . ."

After they work in pairs, ask students to report back about their partner's special skills and abilities to the whole class.

Task 3 Writing a summary

Review what goes in a summary. Summaries can be done in class or assigned as homework tasks. Alternatively, a first draft could be written in class, feedback given, and a second draft written as a homework assignment.

CHAPTER 5 Writing assignment

Go over the questions. Help students select which one they are going to answer. Give students some time in class to think about how they will structure their answer, and give some assistance in their initial organization.

CHAPTER 6

Accounting for Variations in Intelligence

Have students look at the photo of Einstein. Ask them if they recognize this man. Can they tell you why he was such a genius? It might be interesting to tell students that it could not have been because of formal education – Einstein did very badly in high school (dropping out at one point), and he did not do well in college either. Then tell students that so far they have been studying what intelligence is and how it can be measured, and now they are going to consider where intelligence comes from and why some people are more intelligent than others.

1 GENDER AND IQ

PREPARING TO READ

Predicting the content

Explain the different items in the grid. Students should complete the grid and report back to the class what their answers were. Do not tell the students what the correct answers are. Tell them they are about to find out in the reading.

Answers

Who usually does better on tests of the following skills? Check one column for each skill.	Males	Females	No difference
Speaking fluency		✓	
Mathematical ability	✓		
Reading		✓	
General intelligence			✓
Spatial relations (mentally seeing where shapes belong)	✓		
Fine dexterity (moving small object with your hands)		✓	

Skimming for main ideas

Make sure students understand the sentences. Then see if they can predict what the order will be before they read the text. Finally, ask students to skim the text so that they can create a summary of the text by putting sentences *a–d* in the correct order.

Answers

4	*a*
1	*b*
3	*c*
2	*d*

AFTER YOU READ

Task 1 Understanding the organization of a text

This text reads like the classic five-paragraph essay. The purpose of this activity is for students to appreciate how such a text is structured: with an introductory paragraph, three supporting paragraphs, and a concluding paragraph. Further, they are asked to see how certain linking or signal words help the reader negotiate her way through the argument in the text.

1➤ Working individually, students number the text extracts *a–e* according to the order in which they occur in the text.

Answers

3	*a*
5	*b*
1	*c*
4	*d*
2	*e*

2➤ Then have students compare answers with a partner. The final part of the task, where students explain how the words in italics aided them in finding the right order, might best be done as a whole class activity with the teacher guiding the discussion.

Here are some of the points that might be made in this discussion: The first statement, *c*, tells us that there is no difference between men and women in measured IQ. The *at least* tells us that this statement is going to be qualified somewhat. The *however* in statement *e* tells us that we are going to read something about differences between men and women. The *for example* tells us we are about to read some examples of these differences. In statement *a*, the phrase *what this means is that* clearly refers back to something previously stated–the examples–which, as we discover by reading on, must be about differences that are not attributable to education. In statement *d*, the phrase *on the other hand* tells us that we are now going to look at some differences that can be attributed to educational opportunity. Finally, the beginning of statement *b* tells us that a summation of the whole text is about to occur.

Task 2 Reading for detail

Students answer the question, compare answers, and find out what the correct answer is. After doing this, ask students to consider the three items for which no explanation of differences between men and women is given. Ask them if they think the gender differences for these items – reading, verbal fluency, and fine dexterity – might better be explained by environmental factors or innate factors and why.

Answers

      1 reading
ENV *2* math
      3 verbal fluency
      4 fine dexterity
INN *5* spacial relations

---

2 AGE DIFFERENCES AND IQ

PREPARING TO READ

Understanding statistical terms

In this task, students encounter these important statistical terms: *high/low correlation* and *variables*. Make sure students understand them and then see if they can apply them by answering the questions.

Answers

1 Your IQ score when you are 16–18 years old is being correlated with your IQ score when you are 1–15 years old.
2 There is a high correlation after about the age of 10 and a low correlation up to the age of 5.
3 Individuals were given IQ tests at different ages when they were children and then given an IQ test when they were 16–18 years old.

Ask students to predict whether our IQ score changes much over one's lifetime.

Skimming for main ideas

Review what is involved in skimming and surveying a text. Check to make sure that students understand the different items they are looking for.

Answers

  _4_ *a*
  _6_ *b*
  _5_ *c*
  _3_ *d*
  _7_ *e*
  _2_ *f*

AFTER YOU READ

Task 1 Reading for detail

Have students discuss the answers in pairs, then with the whole class.

Sample answers

1 Over 7 years of age
2 Yes: because the cross-sectional method shows younger people getting higher scores than older people. No: because the longitudinal method shows an individual's IQ score changing very little over a lifetime. It depends: because on some specific skills one can detect significant differences in scores over a lifetime.
3 Cross-sectional data: you look at groups of people at one time. Longitudinal data: scientists observe individuals at different periods of time.
4 *Fluid intelligence:* learning a new skill such as how to operate a computer for the first time. *Crystallized intelligence:* solving a problem where a great deal of background knowledge and experience is required, such as when a businessperson has to solve a problem in the workplace.

Task 2 Building vocabulary: Subtechnical vocabulary

Explain the concept of subtechnical vocabulary, that is, vocabulary that is not discipline-specific; it occurs frequently in all academic disciplines. Select some words, from the text or other sources, and ask students whether they are technical words, subtechnical words, or general vocabulary items.

Answers

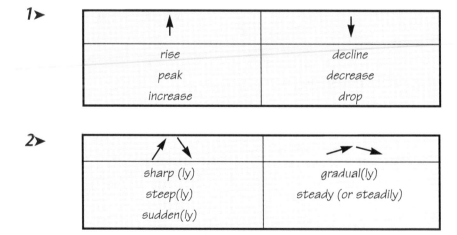

1➤

↑	↓
rise	decline
peak	decrease
increase	drop

2➤

↗↘	↗↘
sharp (ly)	gradual(ly)
steep(ly)	steady (or steadily)
sudden(ly)	

Task 3 Turning written text into a graphic

This task, the previous task, and the following task all revolve around the vocabulary of *increase* and *decrease*. In this task, students decode the vocabulary items in order to create graphs. In Task 4 students encode the language by describing one of the graphs they have created.

Make sure that students understand that the sample graph was created by reading the text closely and that they will now create graphs for other scores in the same way. Then have students draw their graphs and compare their work with a partner.

Have a student come to the front of the class to draw a graph on the board. As he or she draws, read the relevant part of the text to see if the graph accurately reflects the text.

Answers

Vocabulary test scores

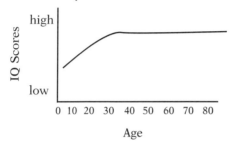

Crystallized intelligence scores

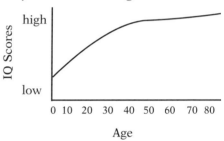

Tests of verbal fluency

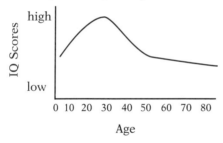

Fluid intelligence scores

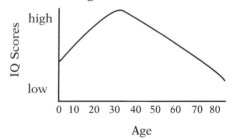

Global IQ scores (longitudinal method)

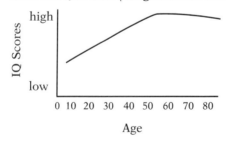

Task 4 Writing: Turning a graph into text

Explain why it is important to be able to describe graphic information in prose form. Students should then describe one of the graphs they created in the previous task.

3 NATURE VERSUS NURTURE

PREPARING TO READ

Thinking about the topic

Much of the research into whether intelligence is inherited or not involves the study of twins. The aim of this activity is to have students think about why this should be so. Put students in small groups for a short discussion. Then discuss the question with the whole class.

Building vocabulary: Guessing meaning from context

This task, which occurs several times in the book, fulfills several functions. First, it exposes students to parts of the text before they read the whole thing, thus facilitating their first reading. Secondly, it helps them understand some of the more difficult vocabulary in the text, and finally it develops an important skill–guessing meaning from context–that they are expected to use every time they confront difficult vocabulary in a text.

AFTER YOU READ

Task 1 Reading for detail

Sample answers

1 There is evidence to support the view that heredity determines intelligence and evidence to support environmental factors, too.
2 It is difficult to define intelligence and we cannot experiment freely on human beings.
3 Raise identical twins in very different environments and see if they emerge with the same IQs, or take two genetically very different babies at birth and raise them in exactly the same environment.
4 One cannot take humans out of their home environment, nor knowingly deprive them for years, for the purposes of a scientific experiment.

Task 2 Punctuation: The use of parentheses

Although this task only deals with parentheses, it makes the point that students need to be aware of how punctuation functions in a text. You might want to take this opportunity to introduce some other aspects of punctuation, for example, dashes, the colon, or the semicolon.

Answers

  =   1 (nature)
  +   2 (and common sense)
  +   3 (and smaller ones)
 REF 4 (Mackintosh, 1986)
  =   5 (environment)
  =   6 (that is, identical twins)

Task 3 Writing

These questions are typical of the questions that students might have to answer in a test on this sort of subject matter. Explain to students that it is worthwhile to practice writing answers to such questions, as though they were preparing for a test.

---

4 *THE STUDY OF TWINS*

PREPARING TO READ

Examining graphic material

Have students study Figure 6.2 and answer the questions before reading the text. From the data in this figure, students can predict what the text is going to be about.

Answers

The subjects (sample answers)

1 An unmarried teenager who has twins might put the twins up for adoption and thus the children end up with different families.

2 When people adopt children because they cannot have children of their own, there will be children who have different birth parents.

3 Identical twins occur when one fertilized egg splits into two. Fraternal twins come from two different eggs being fertilized by two different sperm.

The scores

4 .87

5 .75

6 -.01

7 approximately .22–.82

Reading the conclusion to get the main idea

Tell students that one trick to getting the main idea from a text is to read the concluding section first. Conclusions often summarize the most important information in the whole text. By reading the concluding paragraph in this text, students should be able to piece together what the other paragraphs are going to be about. They should anticipate that the other paragraphs in this text will contain evidence to show that both nurture and nature are responsible for an individual's intelligence.

AFTER YOU READ

Task 1 Interpreting the data

This task revisits the data presented in Figure 6.2. The logic here requires some complex mental processing. This task would not make a good pair work activity. It is probably best done by students working alone, either in class or at home. Even better, the teacher could walk students through each question, helping them arrive at the correct answers.

Answers

1 environment
2 heredity
3 heredity
4 environment

Task 2 Language focus: Expressing parallel change

This task draws attention to a number of structures that occur in the text that have a similar function. In formulaic terms they may be written as follows:

> As X happens, Y also happens.
> The more X happens, the more Y happens.
> X happens, and so does Y.

The transformations students are required to perform in these tasks are difficult. Students should attempt to write them individually in class while you monitor their progress and give help.

Answers

1► *1* The more genetic similarities between subjects increase, the *higher the correlations.*

2 As environments become more extreme, *the differences in IQs also become greater.*

2► *1* As genetic similarities between subjects increase, so *do the correlations in their IQ scores.*

2 As environments become more extreme, so *do the differences in IQ scores.*

CHAPTER 6 Writing assignment

Help students understand the questions and choose one. Put students who have chosen the same question in pairs and have them brainstorm the possible content and organization of their writing assignment.

UNIT 4
Nonverbal Messages

UNIT TITLE PAGE

Elicit some other words for nonverbal messages, such as *nonverbal communication/behavior,* or *body language*. Ask students to try to define this concept. Ask them if they believe it is an important part of human communication.

Tell students to look at the picture. Ask them what they think this man and this woman are talking about. On what do they base their guesses?

Read the unit summary paragraph with the students. Check to be sure that they understand the main concepts.

PREVIEWING THE UNIT

First, have students read the contents page for Unit 4. Then they should work in pairs. Each time they complete a step (give them about five minutes maximum), have a class discussion of their answers.

Chapter 7: Body language

1➤ You could turn this step into a problem-solving activity by saying the phrase, "It's time to go," in the different ways and asking the students to guess which way you were saying it. Students could then work in pairs and do the same thing, that is, say the phrase and have their partners guess which way they said it.

2➤ Make sure students look at the unit contents page to get ideas for their lists.

Chapter 8: The language of touch, space, and artifacts

3➤ To help students do this step, tell or show the class three things that you possess and say how these possessions reveal things about you.

CHAPTER 7

Body Language

1 UNIVERSALS OF NONVERBAL COMMUNICATION

PREPARING TO READ

Previewing text headings

Remind students of the things that a reader should do when surveying a text before reading it. This task will focus on the importance of looking at headings and subheadings as a prelude to reading.

1► Students should read the headings and try to guess the type of information that will be found under them.

2► Let students do this activity individually first. Then put them in pairs to discuss their answers. Monitor their progress and prompt them toward the correct answers.

Answers

4	a
1	b
5	c
3	d
2	e

AFTER YOU READ

Task 1 Analyzing the organization of a text

Many writing instructors teach their students to write paragraphs that start with a topic sentence, continue with support for the topic sentence, and end with a sentence containing some concluding remarks. This task reinforces this method, since it shows students that this is the way that academic texts are often organized.

Answers

1► Like verbal communication, nonverbal communication exists in a context, and that context determines to a large extent the meanings of any nonverbal behaviors.

Nonverbal behaviors . . . usually occur in packages or clusters in which the various verbal and nonverbal behaviors reinforce each other, . . .

Regardless of what one does or does not do, one's nonverbal behavior communicates something to someone. . . .

Nonverbal communication is rule-governed; it is regulated by a system of rules and norms that state what is and what is not appropriate, expected, and permissible in specific social situations.

For some reason . . .we are quick to believe nonverbal behaviors even when these behaviors contradict verbal messages.

2► What constitutes one piece of evidence or two or more is debatable and not always clear. However, it is not really important exactly how many pieces of evidence are in each text. Allow for differences of opinion in doing this activity. The main purpose of the task is for students to be aware that each main idea in this text is supported by evidence.

3►
- _F_ 1
- _T_ 2
- _F_ 3
- _F_ 4
- _T_ 5

Task 2 Language focus: Transitional expressions

After having gone over the information in the task commentary box, have students quickly go through the text, underlining or highlighting as many transitional expressions as they can find in four minutes. Alternatively, you could have students find in the text just those transitional expressions that appear in the exercise. To help students find the expressions, tell them that they occur in the exercise in the same order that they appear in the text.

Students should do the matching activity individually, then compare their answers in pairs. As a follow-up activity, you may want to create a list of other common transitional expressions that can be used to realize each function.

Answers

1	_f_	6	_h_
2	_e_	7	_f_
3	_d_	8	_a_
4	_d_	9	_b_
5	_c_	10	_g_

Task 3 Writing: Using transitional expressions

This task might be done at home as a follow-up to Task 2.

---

2 GESTURAL COMMUNICATION

PREPARING TO READ

Thinking about the topic

This can be an amusing exercise and is best done as a whole class activity. Call on students to show you what gestures they would make in each situation. Encourage cross-cultural comparisons.

The order of events may be a little confusing in this task. First, students only have to read the "What would you do . . . ?" column and demonstrate what they would do, nonverbally, in each of the different situations. Then students read the text. After reading, they return to page 140 to label each pair of gestures according to the category they belong to, and report back to the class.

Answers

1 affect displays
2 regulators
3 emblems
4 adaptors
5 illustrators

AFTER YOU READ

Task 1 Highlighting

Another way to do this task might be to work through one category of gesture at a time. Thus, for example, students would first find and highlight the definition of one category of gesture, then examples of that gesture, and then some commentary about the gesture type. They would then go through the same sequence for the other gesture types.

Task 2 Note-taking practice

Review the note-taking guidelines in the task commentary box on page 101 of the student book. Preteach any other conventions of note-taking that you think would be useful for your students. In particular, you might want to go over some conventional abbreviations and symbols that are used in note-taking.

While students are writing their notes as required in step 1, monitor their progress and suggest improvements. When students do step 2, make sure they only use their notes to do the oral summary. This will allow them to judge the effectiveness of their notes.

Task 3 Thinking critically about the text

1➤ Do this step as a whole class activity. It's entertaining, but it serves to illustrate the point that there are emblematic gestures in some cultures that are unknown to individuals from other cultures.

2➤ Have students work in pairs and then report back to the rest of the class.

3➤ This step can be done as a whole class activity, led by the teacher.

---

3 FACIAL COMMUNICATION

PREPARING TO READ

Make the point that in the previous reading some emblematic gestures were said to be culture-specific. In this text, the notion is that facial expressions are universal, that is, not culture-specific.

Conducting an experiment

1➤ Make sure students understand the meanings of the six different emotions illustrated in the pictures. Students should then decide individually which face expresses which emotion. Compare results in class.

Answers

<u>d</u> happiness
<u>e</u> anger
<u>f</u> fear
<u>b</u> sadness
<u>c</u> disgust
<u>a</u> interest

2➤ This step is an amusing follow-up activity to be done as pair work.

AFTER YOU READ

Task 1 Turning written text into a graphic

This task is designed to appeal to those learners who are more visually oriented. Such learners need to be able to recognize opportunities to display information in a graphic format.

1➤ These facial descriptions all come from paragraph 2 of the text. When students complete the drawing, the face that they have drawn should have a surprised expression on it.

2➤ In order to do this step, students must read paragraph 2 carefully.

Task 2 Building vocabulary: Guessing meaning from context

Another way to execute this task in class is for you to read each passage to the students, prompting them to identify any context clues that will assist them in determining the meaning of the target words. This may be more productive than having the students work on these passages alone.

Task 3 Test-taking: Writing short answers to test questions

1► This task presents an interesting twist to conventional reading comprehension activities. Students are given the questions and the answers! Students enjoy this activity more if you tell them to imagine that they are professors and these are the answers that their students have produced. See how quickly students can turn into sadistic professors, giving low scores to fairly good answers!

Answers

1 A score of about 5 or 6 might be appropriate. The student should have stated what the acronym stands for and been more specific about how the face is divided into parts.
2 A score of about 3 or 4 might be appropriate. The student gives one method. The second method given by the student is incorrect – the judges don't make the facial expressions, these are made by live models whom the judge is observing. The third method is not mentioned at all, which is to have the judge observe someone watching a movie, trying to determine what emotion the movie-watcher is experiencing.
3 A score of 8 or 9 might be appropriate. The student has included the important information about blind children, but misstated somewhat how we know that people from other cultures use the same facial expressions. The experiment mentioned in the text involves people from different cultures interpreting facial expression from photographs, although it is also true that people were asked to pose for certain emotions, too.

2► Make sure students score each answer before they get into groups to justify their scores.

Follow-up: Writing a short answer

The writing follow-up should make students aware of just how difficult it is to give a complete answer in a closed-book, timed exam setting. Even after analyzing these sample answers and discussing them, students will still have a hard time writing a perfect answer.

4 EYE COMMUNICATION

PREPARING TO READ

Building vocabulary: Collocations

1► Explain that *eye contact* is a key concept in this text and can occur in the collocations given. Have students work alone, trying to decide which verb goes into which blank. Have students read the story back to you in class, inserting their choices.

Answers

1➤ I walked into the party . . . I tried to _make_ eye contact . . . he just refused to _return_ my eye contact. He just kept _avoiding_ having any eye contact with me. Then I noticed he _held_ my eye contact for a second or two before _breaking_ it . . . we both looked at each other and _maintained_ eye contact for a full three seconds . . .

2➤
- _g_ 1
- _e_ 2
- _f_ 3
- _b_ 4
- _c_ 5
- _a_ 6
- _d_ 7

Speed reading

Review the guidelines for faster reading on page 36 with the students and make sure that they know exactly what they are to do when they have completed the reading.

AFTER YOU READ

Task 1 Reading for detail

As soon as students have read quickly through the text, they should write down the time it took them to read it. They should then immediately start answering the reading comprehension questions without looking back at the text. Go around the class, looking at students' answers. Tell them which ones they got right and which wrong. Students should then look back at the text for any answers that they missed.

Answers

1 a
2 b
3 b
4 b
5 c
6 a
7 c
8 c
9 a
10 b

Follow-up: How well did you read?

Help students complete the box and calculate their words-per-minute rate and percent correct.

Task 2 Dramatizing the text

In this task, students find out how it feels to break the norms of eye contact. This can be a fun activity, but some of the roles sometimes make students feel uncomfortable, so try not to make any of the rule violation exercises last too long.

Clear a space in the classroom and have students work in pairs, standing up. Designate one person in each pair to be a speaker and the other a listener. Explain what they have to do for each exercise. After a few minutes, stop the rule violation exercise and ask the students to report on how they felt while doing it. Now have the students switch roles to do the next rule violation exercise and so on.

Task 3 Writing a summary

Remind students what goes into a summary. Assign the summary for homework, or do a first draft in class and have students do a rewrite at home.

CHAPTER 7 Writing assignment

Go over the questions with the students in class. Help students decide which question they are going to answer, where to find information that would help them answer the question, and how to go about organizing an answer to the question. Students who choose the same question can work together, thinking through what to include in their answers.

CHAPTER 8

The Language of Touch, Space, and Artifacts

Review the title of the chapter and ask students to predict what sorts of information they will read about and why these topics belong in a unit entitled "Nonverbal Messages."

1 THE MEANINGS OF TOUCH

PREPARING TO READ

Thinking about the topic

Before students do the brainstorming activity, look at the list of verbs of touch and elicit their meanings. Many of these will need to be physically demonstrated to make their meanings clear. After the brainstorming, collect students' ideas on the board.

Skimming for main ideas

Try doing this skimming activity paragraph by paragraph. In other words, have students look at the question that they have to answer for each of the paragraphs listed and then find it as quickly as possible. This should be followed by a discussion of the correct answer in class.

Answers

Paragraph 1	Haptics
Paragraph 3	People who have a relatively close relationship, intimates
Paragraph 4	Yes
Paragraphs 5 and 6	Behaviors, attitudes, feelings
Paragraph 7	Greetings and departures
Paragraph 8	Checking a forehead for a fever

AFTER YOU READ

Task 1 Reading for detail

1► Once students have done the matching activity, they are asked to come up with their own examples. This is a good way to check that they have truly understood the concepts in the text. Probably this is best done as a whole class activity.

Answers

_c_	1
_a_	2
_d_	3
_b_	4
_e_	5

Task 2 Writing

1► Put students in pairs to discuss cross-cultural differences in greeting. Note that touching may not be involved in some of their cultures, in which case, students may refer to bowing or nodding, etc. Make sure students consider variables such as the age, sex, and degree of intimacy of the greeters. You may need to preteach such expressions as: kiss on the cheek, hug, shake hands, etc.

---

2 GENDER AND CULTURAL DIFFERENCES IN TOUCHING

PREPARING TO READ

Thinking about the topic

Tell students that the purpose of this activity is to gain insight into the central question of this text, namely whether peoples' attitudes toward touching and being touched depend on their gender and their cultural background.

1► Before students answer the questionnaire, make sure they understand the context. They have to imagine being touched casually by a friend. *Casually* here means that the touch was not carried out with any particular intention, the friend just happened to place his or her hand there. Also it may be necessary to define *friend* for this activity. *Friend* is being used to mean not a girlfriend or boyfriend, but someone whom one knows well.

2► After completing the questionnaire, students should pair up and show their answers to their partners. If they are paired with someone from the same culture and of the same sex, they should decide if their answers are similar or different and then circle either *similar* or *different* in the appropriate quadrant of the grid. They should then move on, if possible, to someone of the opposite sex and a different culture and go through the same procedure, and so on.

AFTER YOU READ

Task 1 Language focus: The passive

This is a reading comprehension activity disguised as a grammar activity, or vice versa! You will first need to go through a mini grammar lesson on the passive before asking students to complete the sentences with the correct form of the verb.

Answers

1 a
2 a
3 a
4 b
5 b
6 b
7 a
8 b

Task 2 Examining graphic material

In this task, students closely examine Figures 8.1 and 8.2. Make sure students understand how these figures work. In Figure 8.1, the people in the top row are males; in the bottom row, females. Thus, the figure in the top left corner shows how much a mother would touch her son, and the figure in the bottom left shows how much a mother would touch her daughter. At the other end of the diagram, the figure in the top right corner shows how much a boy might be touched by a girl who is a friend, and the figure in the bottom right shows how much a girl might be touched by a boy who is a friend.

Answers

1 a the hands
   b the hands, the legs, and the neck
   c the neck and head
   d the hands and lower arms
   e the feet and lower legs, the hands and arms, the head, neck, and shoulders
2 a the hips and the face
   b none
   c face, mid-torso, hips
   d hands
   e top of the head, face, neck, shoulders, upper arms, hands, hips, and lower legs

Task 3 Writing: Using transitional expressions

Remind students of the importance of using transitional expressions in their writing. Review the transitional expressions used in this exercise *(whereas, how-ever, on the other hand, by contrast, unlike)* and elicit their functions.

   Students are to write sentences based on the information in Figures 8.1 and 8.2.

3 SPACE COMMUNICATION

PREPARING TO READ

Gathering data

Explain to students that in this text they are going to read about the distances people typically keep between themselves and others, depending on the relationship of the people and the nature of the activity that they are engaged in. But first, they are going to do some research of their own. If you are somewhere near where there are people interacting, send your students out in pairs or threes to surreptitiously observe them. (If you are not, then have students do this activity for homework). After five minutes of observing, students should return to class with their reports.

Predicting the content

Ask students to describe what is happening in the four small pictures. Students then guess which type of distance each picture represents, based on the names given to the four types of distance. Have students read the text before you confirm their answers.

Answers

From left to right the pictures show: (c) public distance; (a) intimate distance; (b) personal distance; (c) social distance.

AFTER YOU READ

Task 1 Note-taking: Creating grids

The task commentary box contains important information to go over with your students. It explains how grids can be a useful way for students to organize some types of information in their notes.

Answers

	distance in close phase	*distance in far phase*	*typical relationship between people (in far phase)*	*example of what one can see or smell*	*voice level used*
intimate distance	*touching*	*6–18 inches*	*lovers*	*the other's breath*	*whisper*
personal distance	*1–2 feet*	*2–4 feet*	*friends*	*hair color teeth stains*	
social distance	*4–7 feet*	*7–12 feet*	*colleagues or clients at work*		*louder than normal*
public distance	*12–15 feet*	*more than 25 feet*	*public figures of importance*	*no fine details*	*exaggerated*

Task 2 Conducting an experiment

This task is very similar to the violation of the eye-contact norms task that students did in Section 4 of Chapter 7. Again, students might be uncomfortable doing some of these norm violation exercises, so keep them fairly short and be sensitive to any student's discomfort.

After each norm violation exercise, have the students report to the class how it felt. They can use this information later when they write up the experiment.

---

4 ARTIFACTUAL COMMUNICATION

PREPARING TO READ

Thinking about the topic

Have students make judgments about the people in the illustrations, explaining what influenced their reactions. This could be done as a pair-work activity first, followed by a class discussion.

Scanning

Have students scan the text for the items specified.

Answers

1➤

Sears	an American department store
Volkswagen	a German car company
Levi Strauss	a famous American jeans company
Rolex	a very expensive brand of watch
Alfa Romeo	an Italian car company
Gucci	an Italian company famous for its shoes, handbags, and luggage

2➤

sexy lingerie	something for a woman to wear
weight-lifting machine	something for someone to build body strength
a microscope	a piece of scientific equipment

AFTER YOU READ

Task 1 Inferencing

Before students do the task, explain what *inferencing* means. You could also introduce the vocabulary items *imply* and *read between the lines*. Students need to know that not everything is directly stated in a text and that good readers can read between the lines, working out what the writer left unsaid, or that which the writer implied or inferred.

This task could equally well be carried out as a small group work activity, a pair-work activity or a whole class discussion. Bear in mind that a class discussion gets through the material more quickly, but the other two approaches allow students more opportunities to use the language.

Task 2 Personal writing

Remind students of the rationale for doing personal writing. (See task commentary box on page 73 of student book.) Students could do this writing outside class.

CHAPTER 8 Writing assignment

Go over the three questions with students, making clear what each one involves. Help students understand how the answer to each question might be organized. Students attempting to answer the same questions could meet in pairs to discuss how they might respond to the question.

UNIT 5
Interpersonal Relationships

UNIT TITLE PAGE

Look at the title of the unit with the class. Then look at the picture. Ask students what sorts of relationships they can see illustrated. The following vocabulary set may be elicited or presented: *stranger, acquaintance, close/best friend, girlfriend/boyfriend, lover, husband/wife.*

Read through the unit summary paragraph with the class. Make sure that students understand it.

PREVIEWING THE UNIT

Before students begin answering the questions as pair work, check to be sure they understand the meaning of the titles of each of the sections in Chapters 9 and 10.

Chapter 9: Friendship

1➤ Students should complete the questionnaire individually before they work in pairs to compare their answers and give reasons for their choices. This particular task might work even better as a small group activity, rather than pair work. Have pairs/groups report their conversations to the class.

2➤ This brief pair-work activity should be followed by a whole class discussion.

Chapter 10: Love

1➤ Make sure students understand the proverbs. Ask if they have similar proverbs or sayings in their own countries. See if they can translate them into English. After students briefly discuss the question in pairs, poll the class to see whether more students feel that being different is more appealing than being similar, or the opposite.

2➤ This should be done as a brief pair-work activity, followed by a whole class discussion.

CHAPTER 9

Friendship

1 INITIATING RELATIONSHIPS

PREPARING TO READ

Thinking about the topic

Have students discuss each question in pairs, briefly. Afterwards, have a whole class discussion of their answers.

Highlighting

By doing this activity students will be exposed to some of the most important concepts in the text. As students find the definitions of the key terms, write the terms up on the board and discuss what they mean.

AFTER YOU READ

Task 1 Reading for detail

Make sure students number each step (i.e., each heading), that is, "Examine the Qualifiers" is 1, "Determine Clearance" is 2, etc. Students should then work individually to complete the task. Monitor their progress. Have students compare answers in pairs and then with the whole class. Have students explain how they arrived at each answer.

Answers

5	a
4	b
2	c
1	d
6	e
3	f

Task 2 Building vocabulary: Guessing meaning from context

Students read through the passages and guess the meanings of the words in bold. This can be done as a teacher-led activity or by students working alone. It is not recommended as a pair-work activity.

2 THE NONVERBAL AND VERBAL FIRST ENCOUNTER

PREPARING TO READ

Examining graphic material

Looking at the accompanying photographs before reading a text is a natural thing for a reader to do. Students should be aware that it has a useful function, namely to give them an idea of what they are going to read about and arouse their interest.

After the pair work, have a class discussion of the photograph.

Predicting the content

One way to do this task is to read out the items in the list one at a time, making sure students understand each one. After you read the item, students must write down *R* (for recommended) or *NR* (for not recommended). Then check to see who wrote *R* and who wrote *NR*, before moving on to the next item. If you do the activity this way, it is not really necessary for students to pair up and compare answers.

Don't divulge what will be recommended in the text. You will go over that after students complete their reading.

Answers

NR	1
NR	2
R	3
NR	4
R	5
R	6
R	7
NR	8
R	9
NR	10
R	11
NR	12

AFTER YOU READ

Task 1 Dramatizing the text

In this role play, one student initiates a conversation with another. They role-play two people meeting for the first time. A third student should observe and take notes, recording whether the initiator used good verbal and nonverbal skills. Alternatively, you could select a pair of students to sit in front of the whole class and let the rest of the class be observers.

This task can be extended by having the class or the small groups devise a short observer checklist before the role play begins. The checklist could be a list of questions, such as, "Did the initiator use good eye contact?", "Did the initiator have an open posture (i.e., no arms crossed)?", "Did the initiator start the conversation effectively?", etc. Then the observer just has to check off *yes* or *no* while observing.

After the role play, have the observers report how well they felt the initiators did. Also have those who were approached say whether they felt that following this encounter they would want to befriend the initiators or not.

Ask the students to reflect on whether a role play such as this serves to deepen their understanding of a text more forcefully than a series of reading comprehension questions.

Task 2 Writing a paragraph

The topics for this writing task lend themselves very well to a formulaic three-part paragraph in which there is an opening topic sentence, followed by supporting examples, followed by a concluding statement. Explain to students how the paragraph could be structured before they start writing. Then have them analyze their paragraph after writing (in step 2) and rewrite it (in step 3).

Sample answer

(Topic sentence) There are a number of nonverbal behaviors you should avoid when you first meet someone. (Support 1) For example, it is never a good idea to cross one's arms over one's chest. This creates a barrier between you and the other person. (Support 2) Second, although you want to make eye contact, too much will make the other person feel uncomfortable. (Support 3) Similarly, don't sit too close. (Concluding statement) If you follow this advice you will increase your chances of having a successful first encounter with a stranger whom you would like to meet.

3   FRIENDSHIP FUNCTIONS

PREPARING TO READ

Thinking about the topic

The questions in this task progress from abstract to concrete to highly personal. Particularly with students who are very comfortable together, the questions could be asked in reverse order, finishing with an attempt to define "a friend."

Discussions about friendship can reveal some interesting cross-cultural differences in a multinational class.

Predicting the content

In this task, students are given the names of the five values of friendship that are described in the text. Working from the names only, students are asked to match each name with an extract from the reading which is used to exemplify that value. This activity depends on the students understanding clearly the terms used for the different values of friendship, so go over the glossary carefully with the students, making sure they understand the meanings of the terms.

Students should match the extracts to the five value names, compare with a

partner, and report their answers to the whole class. After reading the text, they
will come back to their answers to see if they made correct predictions.

Answers

_d_	1
_b_	2
_e_	3
_a_	4
_c_	5

AFTER YOU READ

Task 1 Building vocabulary: Synonyms

Go over the information in the task commentary box. Tell your students that
when they write they should try not to repeat vocabulary items, but to see if they
can use synonyms instead.

1➤ Students should search through the text to find the missing words.

Answers

1 to _satisfy_ our needs

2 to _choose_ friends

3 to _become_ friends with people

4 to _help_ us to do something

5 to _maximize_ pleasure

6 to _lessen_ pain

7 to be _depressed_

Task 2 Personal writing

Review the five values of friendship with the students. Let them write for ten
minutes in class. Ask them to report in general terms about the friend that they
wrote about and which of the values of friendship that friend fulfilled for them.
Do not collect or look at the students' writing at any time.

   Tell students that by doing a short personal writing assignment like this, they
may find that they have generated material that might be incorporated into an
essay. Have them look at the writing assignments for Chapter 9 and see if what
they have written might be developed into one of those topics.

4 FRIENDSHIP RULES

PREPARING TO READ

Thinking about the topic

Students who are studying in the United States are often frustrated because they
want to meet Americans but find it difficult to do so. If you are teaching in the

United States, this could be an important discussion for your students, so come to class with some concrete suggestions as to how students can meet Americans, taking into account the particulars of your location and the situations of your students.

EXAMINING GRAPHIC MATERIAL

Clarify any difficult vocabulary in the list of rules in Figure 9.2, such as "stand up for someone" and "confide in someone." Look at the example in the speech bubble, showing what sorts of things students are to come up with in their pair work. When they finish, solicit some of their ideas in a class discussion.

AFTER YOU READ

Task 1 Writing about information in figures

In this activity students learn some simple formulaic language for writing about information in tables. As students write in class, monitor their sentences and suggest improvements. Select students who wrote good sentences to write their answers on the board.

Answers

1➤ Figure A presents the ten most frequently identified activities shared with friends.

The ten most frequently identified activities shared with friends are presented in Figure A.

2➤ (Individuals will vary)

Note that a shared interest in sports often brings friends together.

It is interesting to note that several of the most frequently identified activities shared with friends involve eating and drinking together.

It is worth noting that the number one activity that people identify as something they do with friends is have an intimate talk.

Task 2 Personal writing

Ask your students to reflect on a friendship of theirs that has come to an end. Have students tell the class what happened and which rule of friendship (from Figure 9.3) was broken. Gathering some ideas from the entire class will make it easier for other students to remember a similar friendship breakup. The actual writing could be done as a homework assignment.

CHAPTER 9 Writing assignment

Go over the three questions. Help students decide which one they want to choose and where in the chapter they might find information relevant to their topic. Students who choose the same topic could brainstorm in pairs about how to organize an answer to their question and what sort of information their answer could contain.

CHAPTER 10

Love

There must be many different ways one could introduce this chapter on love: a song, a poem, a short story, an assortment of sayings about love. It doesn't take much to awaken student interest in this topic. For many students it is usually already uppermost in their minds.

1 *SIMILARITY*

PREPARING TO READ

Personalizing the topic

Tell students that the first texts in this chapter deal with the question of what sorts of people we are most attracted to.

1► As a lead-in, have students complete these sentences which explore whom they find attractive and whom they don't find attractive.

In question 1, students are supposed to fill in the blank with actual names of people, not generic types. To make this clear, tell students how you would complete the sentence. Tell students that if their partners give the name of someone they have never heard of, they should ask them to tell them about the person, for example, whether they are a Japanese movie star or an English pop singer, etc.

When students have finished all the pair-work activities, have them share some of the answers in class.

AFTER YOU READ

Task 1 Reading for main ideas

Before students read the text, have them read through the five sentences. After reading, you should expect them to be able to answer these questions very quickly.

Answers

____	1
_b_	2
____	3
_c_	4
_a_	5

Task 2 Writing a one-sentence summary

Ask students to tell you which preposition collocates with each of the three words: *similar, attracted,* and *attitude.*

Sample Answer

We are usually attracted to people that are equal to us in physical attractiveness and who have attitudes and values similar to our own.

Task 3 Personal writing

Remind your students of the sentence frames in the prereading task on page 196 of the student book. Tell them they can include the same sentence structures in their answers, if they wish. Since students have already discussed this question in the prereading task, they should have little trouble finding something to write. Consider giving the writing assignment as homework.

---

2 COMPLEMENTARITY

PREPARING TO READ

Personalizing the topic

Explain to your students that the term *complementarity* must be a technical term in the field of interpersonal relationships, since it is not to be found in the dictionary. The words *complement* and *complementary,* of course, are to be found and provide a key to the title of this section. A *complement* is defined by the *American Heritage Dictionary* as "something that completes, makes up a whole or brings to perfection" and *complementary* as "supplying needs or lacks."

Before students do this task, preteach the word *envy.* Also you may need to do a mini grammar lesson on the special verb forms that should be used in a subordinate clause with the verb *wish* in the main clause. These special forms (*were, could, had,* for example) express the unreal present, or an imaginary or hypothetical state of affairs.

After students write their sentences, instruct them to have them ready to look at again after they have read the text.

AFTER YOU READ

Task 1 Thinking critically about the text

1➤ Students should work in pairs and tell their partners about the sorts of people they may have fallen in love with in the past. According to Reik's theory, the person they describe should have qualities described by them in the prereading task "Personalizing the Topic." Have partners report to the class, and as a whole class assess the validity of Reik's theory.

2► Have students go back to the text and find those parts of the text in which the author shows a bias toward either the similarity principle or the complementarity principle.

Answer

There appear to be three key statements. In the first sentence of the second paragraph, the author uses the word "only" to limit the applicability of the complementarity principle. In the third paragraph, the author writes, "The experimental evidence favors similarity," and the opening sentence of the fourth paragraph reads "Complementarity finds less support."

Task 2 Building vocabulary: Antonyms

Students should do the exercise individually, compare their answers in pairs, and check the answers with the whole class.

Answers

1 submissive
2 extrovert
3 aggressive
4 placid
5 woman

3 TYPES OF LOVE

PREPARING TO READ

Building vocabulary: Learning word clusters

See how many of the vocabulary items students can fill into the blanks without the use of a dictionary or your assistance. Then go over the answers together, clarifying some of the more difficult vocabulary.

Answers

1 a j n
2 d i k
3 f m o
4 e h l
5 b c g

AFTER YOU READ

Task 1 Reading for detail

Although this is a fairly long text, students need not take too long to answer this question, since the differences between the different types of lovers is fairly transparent.

Answers

c	1
d	2
a	3
e	4
b	5

Task 2 Test-taking: Making lists to study from

Although this is called a test-taking task, it also involves note-taking. Explain to your students why one would make a list, such as the sample list in Step 1, before taking a test.

Students make their own lists in step 2 and compare their notes for completeness with a student who studied the same part of the text as they did. They then partner up with a student who studied a different part of the text and give an oral summary of the type of lover that they studied.

Step 4 is optional. It may be omitted if time is limited. It gives students additional practice in anticipating test questions and illustrates how test question anticipation may also be done by looking at notes, rather than looking at the text itself.

Task 3 Personalizing the topic

Depending on your class, you may find the final task for this section to be too personal to be done with the whole class or as pair work. If that is the case, explain how to complete and score the questionnaire and then have students do it at home. There need not be any sharing of the results of the questionnaire afterward. For those classes in which you feel there would be no discomfort about sharing scores, students can reveal how many points they got for each type of lover.

---

4 GENDER DIFFERENCES IN LOVING

PREPARING TO READ

Predicting the content

Teach some of the key vocabulary that is necessary to do this task and some related vocabulary: *to be infatuated with someone, to have a crush on someone, to fall in love with someone, to be head over heels in love with someone*, etc.

Students should work in pairs and make their predictions. They then compare their predictions with another pair of students and discuss together how they would have answered the questions.

Have the groups report their predictions, and their personal information if they are comfortable doing so. Tell students that they will find out what the correct answers are after they finish reading.

Speed reading

Review the guidelines for faster reading in the task commentary box on page 36 of the student book and also make sure students know what to do as soon as they have finished reading. For this speed-reading task the postreading comprehension exercise is different from what students have done previously. Before students start their reading, have them look at Task 1 on page 211 of the student book. Go over how they are supposed to fill out the grid. Also quickly review the questions they will be answering.

AFTER YOU READ

Task 1 Reading for detail

Students should fill out the grid. Then go around the class telling students which answers they got right and which wrong. Students can then go back to the text to find out what the correct answers are.

	Men	*Women*
1 They are said to love more intensely.	✓	
2 They show more love for same-sex friends.		✓
3 They have more infatuations.		✓
4 For a student between the ages of 18–24, the average number of times in love is less than 2.	✓	✓
5 The median age of first infatuation is between the ages of 13 and 14.	✓	✓
6 The median age of first falling in love is between the ages of 17 and 18.	✓	✓
7 More than 50 percent say they would not marry someone if they were not in love with him/her.	✓	
8 They more often cause the breakup of a relationship by becoming interested in another partner.		✓
9 They tend to remember only pleasant things after a breakup.	✓	✓
10 After a breakup they tend to daydream more about the lost partner.	✓	

Task 2 Thinking critically about the text

For questions 1 and 2, students discuss their reactions to the information in the text from a personal and cross-cultural perspective. To do question 3, they need to look carefully at the text to re-create the possible questions. In question 4, they answer them. Share the questions and the answers with the entire class.

Sample questions

1 If a boy/girl had all the qualities you desired in a mate, would you marry this person even if you were not in love with him/her?
2 If you are married, how would you describe your love for your husband/wife?
3 If you have ever broken up with someone in a relationship, who caused the break up?
4 If you have ever broken up with someone, what was the reason for the breakup: mutual loss of interest or your or your partner's romantic interest in another person?
5 After breaking up with someone, do you tend to have pleasant or unpleasant memories of the relationship?
6 After a breakup, do you daydream about the lost partner?

Task 3 Writing a summary

Review how to write a summary. Have students write a first draft in class. Give feedback and have them rewrite the summary for homework.

CHAPTER 10 Writing assignment

Go over the different questions in class and help students select the one that they would most like to answer. Discuss where in the chapter they might find information relevant to their topic. Put students who are going to answer the same topic in pairs and have them brainstorm the sort of information they might include in their writing and the way it might be organized.

CONTENT QUIZ ANSWERS

Unit 1

Part 1

1 _T_
2 _T_
3 _F_
4 _T_
5 _F_
6 _T_

Part 2

1 b
2 a
3 d
4 c

Part 3

1 The study of how mental events affect the immune system or, how the mind can influence the body.
2 Smokers who smoke and drink coffee at the same time might be able to give up smoking if they also give up coffee drinking, because it is a stimulus which makes them think about smoking.
3 Do your exercise program in a group or with a friend or spouse and build exercise into your everyday life, such as walking up stairs rather than taking an elevator.

Part 4

1 Reference should be made to Type A people being hard-working, driven, intense, more likely to get into challenging situations. Reference should also be made to Type B people as being more relaxed, less achievement-oriented, more concerned with personal satisfaction.
2 Being "well" should be defined as being in the best health possible for each individual, achieved by healthy diet, exercise, and regular check-ups, etc. On the other hand, "ill" should be defined as having an active diagnosable complaint. Thus even if you are not ill, you are not necessarily well.

Unit 2

Part 1

1 _F_
2 _T_
3 _F_
4 _T_
5 _T_
6 _F_

Part 2

1 b
2 c
3 d
4 b

Part 3

1 Adolescence can be defined physically (how an individual's body changes), psychologically (how an individual's thought processes, feelings, and behaviors change), and socially (how an individual's social status changes).
2 In adulthood individuals learn how to become independent of their parents; on the other hand, they develop new intimate relationships, with friends or a spouse, and have to learn how to live together with these people.
3 The birth rate is going down and people are living longer.

Part 4

1 Reference should be made to self-esteem problems for late-blooming boys and the advantages for early-blooming girls and boys. A full answer would also mention that late- blooming girls are at a disadvantage during adolescence (in terms of self-esteem), but that this may turn out to be an advantage later, since they can concentrate better on studies and other interests.
2 A good answer would produce evidence from the reading to show that the elderly are not as lonely, financially poor, mentally and physically in poor health, or as inactive as myth might have us believe.

Unit 3

Part 1

1 F
2 T
3 F
4 T
5 T
6 T

Part 2

1 d
2 b
3 a
4 a

Part 3

1 Intelligence defined operationally might depend on a score on an intelligence test; a theoretical definition would refer to how well an individual solves problems, for example.

2 Alfred Binet devised an intelligence test in France at the beginning of the twentieth century. A professor at Stanford, Lewis Terman, translated the test into English and revised it.

3 Any four of the following six:

good psychomotor skills
high ability in performing arts
creative thinking ability
skill in one particular academic area, e.g., math
leadership skills
mental intelligence as measured on an intelligence test

Part 4

1 The answer should include the following points: (1) Yes, because people in different age groups get different scores on IQ tests; (2) No, because when compared to other people of the same age there is little relative change in IQ scores; (3) It depends, because when you look at a variety of different skills you see that as we get older we score better on some tests and fall away on others.

2 The answer should include the fact that it is morally unacceptable to experiment on humans in the way that one would have to were the perfect experiment designed. For example, some individuals would have to be deprived of a comforting and stimulating environment, others would have to be taken away from their families and put in other families.

Unit 4

Part 1

1 F
2 T
3 T
4 T
5 F
6 T

Part 2

1 c
2 b
3 c
4 c

Part 3

1 When someone is unsatisfied with another person they may give as a gift something which unconsciously suggests how the gift-giver would like the recipient to change. For example, a woman may give some weightlifting equipment to a man she sees as not muscular enough.

2 Two of the following four:

To monitor feedback, i.e., see what effects one's words are having
To signal a conversational turn, i.e., to show it is another person's turn to speak
To signal the nature of a relationship, i.e., how intimate two people are
To compensate for physical distance, i.e., use more eye contact when farther, less when nearer

3 In many cultures touching rarely occurs, except during some ritual such as when two people meet or leave each other. For example, in many cultures people shake hands when they meet.

Part 4

1 A complete answer may refer to the fact that each culture has rules for eye contact, touching, and interpersonal distance. Examples may be given of each. Then reference may be made to how it feels when any of these rules are broken. Reference may also be made to gestures and facial expressions. Even though these tend to be less culture-specific, there are still rules: We expect certain gestures and not others, and we expect certain facial expressions to convey particular emotions.

2 Reference should be made to studies about gender differences in touching in the United States. Women are permitted to touch each other in public (give examples) more than men. In private, however, some studies have found that men and women touch about the same (except for the touching behavior of mothers and fathers: mothers do more touching and are touched more). Other studies have found that women touch more, and like to be touched more. The answer should also make clear that gender differences in touching will vary from culture to culture. For example, touching behavior in Japan and the United States can be shown to have numerous differences.

Unit 5

Part 1

1 T
2 F
3 F
4 F
5 T
6 T

Part 2

1 d
2 d
3 b
4 a

Part 3

1 When something good happens we get pleasure by sharing the good news with friends, and when something bad happens we feel less pain by sharing the bad news, too.

2 Three from this list of six:

Avoid cliched or trite opening lines

Do not be overly negative

Avoid talking too intimately about oneself and one's deepest feelings

Do not ask yes/no questions

Do not answer questions with short yes/no answers

Do not ask too many personal questions

3 The matching hypothesis states that people are more likely to date and marry others who are similar to them in terms of their physical attractiveness.

Part 4

1 Reference could be made to the research showing men to be more romantic about marriage than women, and less likely to cause a breakup by finding another partner. Also girls are infatuated and fall in love as teenagers at a slightly younger age and slightly more times.

2 A complete answer will discuss some of the functions of friendship, in particular the concept that friends serve to maximize pleasure and minimize pain. Secondly, reference should be made to some of the rules that should be observed to maintain a friendship (stand up for a friend in his or her absence, for example), and to behaviors that can lead to the breakup of a friendship (being intolerant of a friend's friends, for example).

UNIT 1   Content Quiz

Part 1   True/False questions (12 points)

Decide if the following statements are true (T) or false (F).

_____ *1* Stress reactions can cause the immune system not to function properly.

_____ *2* The leading cause of death in the United States is heart disease.

_____ *3* No study has ever found a link between being depressed and dying of cancer.

_____ *4* There is a lower rate of heart disease in Japan than there is in the Japanese American community in the United States.

_____ *5* Despite all the health warnings, the number of smokers in the United States continues to rise each year.

_____ *6* Even moderate levels of regular exercise reduce the chances of one's developing heart disease.

Part 2   Multiple choice questions (12 points)

Circle the best answer from the choices listed.

1 What do all stressful events have in common?
   a They lead to suffering, illness, or pain.
   b They interfere with our everyday life or routine.
   c They give rise to feelings of anger or fear.
   d They lead to alarm reaction, resistance, and collapse.

2 Which of the following would *not* be good advice to help an individual cope with a stressful event?
   a Think of the stressful event as a danger and a threat.
   b Try to predict what is going to happen.
   c Gain some control over what is going to happen.
   d Think of the stressful event as an opportunity to prove your ability.

3 Which of the following would *not* be identified as a risk factor for heart disease, particularly for a Type B personality?
   a A high cholesterol level
   b Smoking
   c A family history of heart disease
   d A stressful job

4 According to the results of one study, women who have been diagnosed with cancer should _____.
   a react calmly and accept the situation
   b receive electric shock treatment that they can control
   c become angry and express their emotion
   d exercise regularly

Part 3   Short answer questions (12 points)

Write a short answer to each of the following questions. In most cases no more than a sentence is required.

1 What is psychoimmunology?

2 Describe how *stimulus control* could be used to help someone who wants to give up smoking.

3 What advice might a psychologist give to someone in order to help him or her stay on a fitness or exercise program?

Part 4 One paragraph or short essay answer (14 points)

Choose one of the following topics and write a paragraph or short essay. Use a separate sheet of paper.

1 Type A and Type B personalities
2 The difference between being "not ill" and being "well"

UNIT 2 Content Quiz

Part 1 True/False questions (12 points)

Decide if the following statements are true (T) or false (F).

_____ *1* Psychologists all agree that adolescence is a negative period of great turmoil and stress.

_____ *2* The growth spurt of early adolescence usually occurs in girls at an earlier age than it does in boys.

_____ *3* According to Levinson, young adulthood is a relatively calm period of life, free of stress and difficult decisions.

_____ *4* Successful and unsuccessful suicide attempts among the young increased significantly during the 1970s and 1980s in the United States.

_____ *5* According to psychologist David Buss, we are most likely to marry someone who is similar to us in many ways.

_____ *6* The older people become, the more they begin to fear death.

Part 2 Multiple choice questions (12 points)

Circle the best answer from the choices listed.

1 Which of the following best describes the democratic parental style?
  a Parents act as friends and do not impose any rules or limits.
  b Parents act as experts, give advice, and allow a certain degree of freedom, but do set limits.
  c Parents are supportive, but interfere as little as possible in their children's lives.
  d Parents are quite strict and are not willing to discuss any of the rules they impose on their children.

2 Which of the following is the accurate ranking of the leading causes of death among teenagers in the United States?
  a Suicide, disease, murder, accidents
  b Accidents, suicide, disease, murder
  c Accidents, murder, suicide, disease
  d Murder, suicide, accidents, disease

3 When men and women are asked to rank the most important characteristics in a mate, which do they both rank as numbers 1 and 2?
  a (1) kindness and understanding, and (2) physical attractiveness
  b (1) intelligence, and (2) exciting personality
  c (1) physical attractiveness, and (2) intelligence
  d (1) kindness and understanding, and (2) intelligence

4 Which of the following is not one of the seven major tasks one must face in middle adulthood?
  a Adjusting to aging parents
  b Deciding what sort of career one should devote one's life to
  c Achieving adult social and civic responsibility
  d Developing leisure-time activities

Part 3 Short answer questions (12 points)

Write a short answer to each of the following questions. In most cases no more than a sentence is required.

1 What are the three ways of defining adolescence?

2 "Psychologically speaking, adulthood is marked by two possibilities that at first seem contradictory: (1) independence . . . [and] (2) interdependence." Explain this statement from Chapter 4, Section 1, "Early Adulthood."

3 Give two reasons why the percentage of elderly people in the United States is increasing.

Part 4 One paragraph or short essay answer (14 points)

Choose one of the following topics and write a paragraph or a short essay. Use a separate sheet of paper.

1 The problems and benefits associated with being an early or a late bloomer during adolescence
2 The myths of old age

UNIT 3   Content Quiz

Part 1   True/False questions (12 points)

Decide if the following statements are true (T) or false (F).

_____ *1* The first intelligence test was designed by David Wechsler.

_____ *2* The Terman study is an example of a longitudinal study.

_____ *3* The Terman study found that there is no difference between children with high IQs and other children when judged by the degree of their success in adult life.

_____ *4* The fact that males generally do better than females in tests of mathematics appears to be due to increased educational opportunities for males rather than to innate differences.

_____ *5* The correlation of the IQ scores of 12 year olds with their adult IQ scores is high.

_____ *6* Two brothers who are raised apart are less likely to have the same IQ than if they had been raised together.

Part 2   Multiple choice questions (12 points)

Circle the best answer from the choices listed.

1 Intelligence may be defined as _____.
  a everything you know
  b the ability to solve problems
  c the ability to learn from experience
  d all of the above

2 Alfred Binet developed his intelligence test because the French government wanted _____.
  a to be able to identify the best and brightest students at an early age
  b him to find out why some children did not do well in school
  c him to participate in a joint study of intelligence with Stanford University
  d him to recommend changes to the French educational system

3 Someone who has good verbal and quantitative skills (which may be influenced by schooling) may be said by a psychologist to have _____.
  a good crystallized abilities
  b good fluid analytic abilities
  c good performance skills
  d a good memory

4 In tests of which one of the following areas do males perform better than females?
  a Spatial relations
  b Reading
  c Speaking
  d Fine dexterity

Part 3   Short answer questions (12 points)

Write a short answer to each of the following questions. In most cases no more than a sentence is required.

1 Give an example of an operational definition of intelligence and an example of a theoretical definition of intelligence.

2 How did the Stanford-Binet intelligence test get its name?

3 What are four different areas in which someone might be described as gifted, according to the United States Office of Education report (1972)?

Part 4 One paragraph or short essay answer (14 points)

Choose one of the following topics and write a paragraph or short essay. Use a separate sheet of paper.

1 Does intelligence change as you get older? Why is the answer to this question "Yes," "No," and "It depends"?

2 Why is it so difficult to design an experiment to determine whether genetic or environmental factors are more important in determining an individual's intelligence?

UNIT 4   Content Quiz

Part 1   True/False questions (12 points)

Decide if the following statements are true (T) or false (F).

_____ *1* Eye contact rules and norms appear to be universal, that is they are the same all around the world.

_____ *2* Touching rules and norms appear to be different in different cultures.

_____ *3* Facial expressions appear to be universal, that is they are the same all around the world.

_____ *4* We are more likely to judge an individual positively if the person has dilated pupils.

_____ *5* Emblem gestures appear to be universal, that is the same expression communicates the same emotion all around the world.

_____ *6* The closer you are to a stranger, the more likely you are to avoid eye contact.

Part 2   Multiple choice questions (12 points)

Circle the best answer from the choices listed.

1 Two coworkers are talking at an office party. What distance are they likely to keep between them?

a intimate
b personal
c social
d public

2 The study of the way people gesture and use body movements to communicate is called _____.

a haptics
b kinesics
c proxemics
d paralanguage

3 When a nurse touches a patient while taking his blood pressure, to which category of touch does this action belong?

a control
b positive affect
c task relatedness
d playfulness

4 Scratching one's nose when it itches is an example of _____ gesture.

a an emblem
b an illustrator
c an adaptor
d a regulator

Part 3   Short answer questions (12 points)

Write a short answer to each of the following questions. In most cases no more than a sentence is required.

1 What is a Pygmalion gift? Give an example.

2 Mark Knapp proposed four major functions of eye communication. Name and describe two of them.

3 Define *ritual touching* and give examples.

Part 4 One paragraph or short essay answer (14 points)

Choose one of the following topics and write a paragraph or a short essay. Use a separate sheet of paper.

1 Explain why nonverbal communication can be regarded as *rule-governed behavior.*

2 Gender differences in touching

UNIT 5   Content Quiz

Part 1   True/False questions (12 points)

Decide if the following statements are true (T) or false (F).

_____ *1* During a first encounter it is a good idea to give the other person plenty of opportunities to talk about himself or herself.

_____ *2* A good opening line when you see someone in a bar or disco would be "Haven't I seen you here before?"

_____ *3* Research shows that people who marry people who are very different from themselves are less likely to get divorced than people who marry people very similar to themselves.

_____ *4* The ludic lover is most interested in a long, peaceful, and satisfying relationship, similar to a friendship.

_____ *5* Most people, both men and women, claim to have fallen in love for the first time when they were teenagers.

_____ *6* More women than men said they would marry someone they weren't in love with.

Part 2   Multiple choice questions (12 points)

Circle the best answer from the choices listed.

1 Which of the following nonverbal behaviors is *not* recommended on a first encounter?
  a Getting fairly close physically
  b Maintaining steady eye contact
  c Smiling
  d Sitting with arms folded across the chest

2 If a friend helps you find a new job, this is an example of his or her _____ value.
  a stimulation
  b ego-support
  c affirmation
  d utility

3 Which type of lover focuses more than any other type on the physical attractiveness of their partner?
  a The manic lover
  b The erotic lover
  c The ludic lover
  d The storgic lover

4 According to Chapter 9, Section 1, "Initiating Relationships," the first three steps in a first encounter should be to first _____.
  a examine qualifiers, then determine clearance, and thirdly, look for free information
  b look for free information, then examine qualifiers, and thirdly, determine clearance
  c determine clearance, then look for free information, and thirdly, examine qualifiers
  d look for free information, then determine clearance, and thirdly, examine qualifiers

Part 3   Short answer questions (12 points)

Write a short answer to each of the following questions. In most cases no more than a sentence is required.

1 Explain how friendship can serve both to maximize pleasure and minimize pain.

2 What are three verbal behaviors that someone initiating a conversation should avoid?

3 Define the *matching hypothesis*.

Part 4 One paragraph or short essay answer (14 points)

Choose one of the following topics and write a paragraph or a short essay. Use a separate sheet of paper.

1 Gender differences in loving
2 How to maintain a good friendship